THE NEW CHINESE

THE NEW CHINESE
HOW THEY ARE SHAPING AUSTRALIA

BARRY LI

WILEY

First published in 2017 by John Wiley & Sons Australia, Ltd
42 McDougall St, Milton Qld 4064

Office also in Melbourne

Typeset in 12.5/14.5 pt ITC Berkeley Oldstyle Std

© John Wiley & Sons Australia, Ltd 2017

The moral rights of the author have been asserted

National Library of Australia Cataloguing-in-Publication data:

Creator:	Li, Tian (Barry), author.
Title:	The New Chinese: How they are shaping Australia / Barry Li.
ISBN:	9780730351870 (pbk.)
	9780730351887 (ebook)
	9780730345336 (custom)
Notes:	Includes index.
Subjects:	Chinese Australians.
	Chinese — Australia — History.
	Chinese Australians — Cultural assimilation.

Cover design by Kathy Davis/Wiley

Cover images: The empty China passport (koosen /Shutterstock); Travel stamps background (Tupungato /Shutterstock)
Internal images: Travel stamps background (Tupungato /Shutterstock)

Printed in Singapore by C.O.S. Printers Pte Ltd

10 9 8 7 6 5 4 3 2 1

Disclaimer

The material in this publication is of the nature of general comment only, and does not represent professional advice. It is not intended to provide specific guidance for particular circumstances and it should not be relied on as the basis for any decision to take action or not take action on any matter which it covers. Readers should obtain professional advice where appropriate, before making any such decision. To the maximum extent permitted by law, the author and publisher disclaim all responsibility and liability to any person, arising directly or indirectly from any person taking or not taking action based on the information in this publication.

To my father, Yanjiang Li, and my mother, Xiaoyu Gao,
who brought me into this world, then showed me the way
to live life freely and honestly.

CONTENTS

ABOUT THE AUTHOR

Barry Li was born in China a few years after the end of the Cultural Revolution, living 22 years in Qitaihe, Suzhou and later Beijing before deciding to complete his higher education studies in Australia. After graduation and a few years' work in Australia, in 2010 he returned with his wife, Zhen, to China, to find a country transformed by an economic boom that showed no sign of slowing. Finding no place for themselves in the new China, the following year they returned to Australia to create a permanent home in Sydney.

Barry has a bachelor's degree in Economics from the University of International Business and Economics (UIBE), Beijing, and a Master of Commerce degree from Macquarie University in Australia. He is currently pursuing further studies at the University of New South Wales.

Besides being a Certified Practising Accountant and auditor, he is a long-term volunteer for CPA Australia and currently chairs the CPA NSW Young Professionals Committee. He and Zhen have two young sons.

ACKNOWLEDGEMENTS

I'd like to sincerely thank the following people who made this book possible.

First, my mentor, Glenda Korporaal, who was kind enough to coach me over several months on writing a book in English. Christine Brooks and Samantha Berry, from the University of New South Wales, found me my amazing mentor. Jan Stewart, from Hub Australia, and successful author Gabrielle Dolan, from Thought Leaders Global, introduced me to Wiley, the publisher of my dreams. I can't thank them enough for helping me so generously and selflessly.

Wiley staff members Lucy Raymond, Clare Dowdell, Chris Shorten and Ingrid Bond worked hard in the background to turn my manuscript into a real book. I feel they devoted so much energy to this book not because it will become the next bestseller, but because they value cultural diversity and respect the story of an ordinary migrant like me. I greatly appreciate that generosity. I'm even more grateful to my editor, Jem Bates, who worked so hard to correct my poor grammar and wording, but always gave me recognition and encouragement.

Writing this book turned out to be like running a marathon with no previous training. Without the tremendous support of my boss at Audit Office of New South Wales, Renee Meimaroglou, the journey simply wouldn't have begun. When

I showed a draft of the first chapter to my friend Sissi Qian, her comments (including words like 'fabulous' and 'classic'!) inspired me to continue the journey. Once I had a complete draft, the challenge of finding a publisher again weighed me down, until Ann Persky from CPA Australia, who has managed the CPA library for decades, looked it over and declared she found it very interesting. I simply would not have finished the journey without all this encouragement.

My idea of writing a book about the new China and the new Chinese people was born from reading *Mao's Last Dancer* by Cunxin Li, who has told a great story of his own incredible journey and who vividly depicted communist China *prior* to Deng Xiaoping's reform and opening up policy. I refer in the book to other individuals who have inspired me, whether they be people around me, such as Jane Lu of Showpo, or public figures I have never met in person, such as Australia's former prime minister Kevin Rudd; Jack Ma, the founder of Alibaba; and famous Chinese journalist Chai Jing. Thank you all for enriching my life and my book.

Lastly, my lovely wife, Zhen, and my wonderful children, Nathan and Alexander. You have all made sacrifices so I could carve out the time to write this book. I'm here to give back to you for the rest of my life.

FOREWORD
BY GLENDA KORPORAAL

The rise of modern China, with the opening up of its economy, has been one of the most important developments in our lifetime. In a few short decades, China has become the second largest economy in the world. This has had a major impact on the rest of the world and seen a refocus of political, economic and social relations with Asia.

China has played a key role in Australia's own economic fortunes, becoming its largest trading partner and a major investor. But an equally important influence in recent times has been the arrival of thousands of young Chinese from mainland China to study in Australia and then to seek their future here.

Hardworking, law-abiding and aspirational, these young, educated 'new Chinese'—many from one-child families whose parents have experienced extreme hardship—have been part of the latest wave of migrants to Australia. Studying, working and now buying their first homes, they are quietly putting down roots in Australia and becoming part of our society.

Australia has a rich history of absorbing people from all around the world, including my own Dutch father and English grandfather. But language and cultural differences, and the sheer adaptability of the 'new Chinese', have meant that few

Australians have sought to understand the history, motivations and dreams of this latest generation of migrants.

While much has been written about Australia's growing relationship with China, Li and his generation of migrants provide an important personal bridge to modern China that has yet to be fully recognised. They are shaping Australia as students, employees, consumers and friends. Many of them have made Australia their home and are now contributing significantly to our society, yet few Australians understand the long journey that has brought them here.

With honesty, clarity and a passion for his new homeland, Barry Li has sought to tell his story and explain the forces behind his generation, and especially those who have chosen to come here.

As he has carved out a new life for himself and his young family, Li has developed a strong affection for Australia. Viewing China through the eyes of an 'ordinary' new Australian, he is also astonished at the impact of the rapid economic and social changes that have been going on in his homeland in recent years. In this book he seeks to explain some of these tectonic changes, how they have affected his generation of young Chinese and what it all means for Australia.

Written from his own 'grassroots' perspective, Li's story and his observations and thoughts provide valuable insights into an important and exciting force for change in Australia. The 'new Chinese' are changing the world. Li's book is an important window into how they are changing Australia.

Glenda Korporaal
Associate Editor — Business
The Australian
January 2017

INTRODUCTION

This is a true story. It is a story about me, a very ordinary Chinese man. I was never physically tortured or persecuted by the 'evil communist regime', but still I had to 'escape' from China for a better life. It also tells the story of what has happened inside China since the Cultural Revolution, especially during the past 30 years when it has grown from one of the poorest developing countries to the world's second largest economy. Finally, it tells the story of how a new-generation Chinese migrant finds his place in Australian society and works towards his Australian dream.

Let me begin with a few special moments in my life. In September 2011 my wife Zhen and I landed at Sydney's Kingsford Smith Airport after our 'exodus' from China. All we had with us that day were two suitcases of clothes—and a six-months-pregnant belly. We had nowhere to live, no relatives, no jobs and not much in savings. No one came to the airport to welcome us. We rented a small car from Budget and bought two mobile phone numbers with the cheapest plan from Vodafone. Then we drove to the Ibis Budget Hotel, where I had booked us a room online.

After dinner at McDonald's Zhen was quite tired. She had vomited many times during the 11-hour red-eye flight. I knew she had no appetite but was forcing herself to eat for the sake of the baby growing inside her. When I put our dirty clothes in the coin-operated washing machine in the laundry and returned to our small room, she was already asleep in the not-so-comfortable bed. She had to sleep on her side because her belly was so big. Looking at her back, I almost started to cry. I felt so bad that I had put her through this journey, and the worst part was I had no idea where I was heading. But I had no time to cry. I wiped my eyes and turned on my laptop. I needed to find somewhere for us to live, some place we could afford, yet I had no idea if anyone would even rent to a jobless couple like us.

One week later we bought a 12-year-old car and moved into a small apartment in Westmead. In a day I had assembled all the furniture from IKEA, including a baby cot and a nappy-change table. I was exhausted, but I felt overwhelmingly relieved that we finally had a place for the baby if it decided to come early. I could also cook nutritious and healthy homemade meals for Zhen. Most importantly, we were no longer homeless. When everything was assembled I was ready to drop. I fell asleep almost instantly.

The next day Zhen had her first check-up at the Westmead hospital. The baby was fine. I had yet to find a job, but Zhen didn't seem too worried. She had strong faith in me, or maybe she just didn't want to show her anxiety and put extra pressure on me. I told her if I couldn't find a job in accounting, I would take on *any* work to make sure she and the baby had everything they needed. I even started to apply for cleaning jobs advertised in the local newspaper.

I didn't find a job in accounting—it wasn't long after the global financial crisis, and very few businesses were hiring—but I found a commission-based sales job. It didn't offer much job security, but I finally started making money again. Zhen was so happy. After paying the rent and basic living expenses, we spent what was left on baby clothes, nappies and a pram.

One early December night Zhen's contractions started. I was so excited. We rushed to the hospital, and our 48-hour battle began. I could never truly feel her pain, but after a day of her screaming, I could see Zhen was exhausted. I too felt drained. When the doctor told me the baby was not going to come out naturally, that they needed to perform a caesarean section and there was a chance she could die, I almost collapsed. Zhen was in great pain and clutched my hands tightly. I was afraid I might lose her that night.

My son was born at midnight. In the operating theatre, when I held him for the first time, I finally started to cry. I just could not hold it in anymore. He was so small, so precious, so ugly and yet so beautiful. Zhen had lost a litre of blood during the birth, but she was okay. I felt blessed. Besides my son, a new man was born that night—me. For the first time in my life, I understood what it felt like to be a man and a father.

In the morning I sent a text message to my parents in Beijing, telling them their first grandson had been born and everyone was well. Although they were happy with the news, I knew they had still not forgiven me for leaving China as I had. I didn't care, because now I was a father too, and I knew I was doing the right thing for my wife and child. With or without my parents' blessings, I would ensure my son had the best life possible.

The next morning I received a phone call from an HR agent, who had a job offer for me. It was a full-time telemarketing role with an IT company. She wasn't at all sure I would be interested as it was just a 12-month contract and paid only $50000. I said yes, definitely *yes*! I was so happy to secure 12 months' income for my new family. It was definitely the most exciting job offer I had ever received.

Three months later Zhen found a contract job near home. We were lucky that her mother came from China to help look after our boy. Zhen went to work in the morning, came home at lunchtime to breastfeed, then went back to work again in the afternoon. With her income we started saving, because we hoped one day to buy our own property.

Six months later still my parents came to Australia to meet their grandson for the first time. I could see they loved him, although they were still very disappointed in me for deserting China and then taking on some 'embarrassing' cold-calling sales job when they had spent so much on my professional education in accounting.

When I completed the telemarketing contract, the company asked me to stay on in sales, but I knew it was time to move back into accounting, a career that offered me a better future given my educational background. After a long search I finally found an entry-level auditor job with PricewaterhouseCoopers (PwC), the world's largest accounting firm. It was a dream job for any accounting graduate. I was some 10 years older than my peers, who had just graduated from university, but I knew it was never too late to start something great.

Another year passed and Zhen found a better job. We finally had enough savings to put down a deposit on our first home. It was a very old unit (older than we were ourselves) in the northern suburbs of Sydney, but we felt so happy when we moved into the first home we had owned. A few months after we moved, Zhen was pregnant again. About the time my second child was born, I was promoted at work.

Last year I moved to Audit Office of New South Wales as an experienced financial auditor. Zhen landed a job as a financial analyst. We finally had the jobs and the life every new migrant dreamed of. When we returned to Beijing with two lovely children over Christmas, although they did not say as much, I knew my parents had finally accepted that I had made the right decision in leaving China five years ago.

So why did I have to escape from China in the first place? To answer that question, I need to fill in some of the background to my own story, which is my aim in this book.

In chapter 1, I introduce some more stories of the new Chinese, in particular from my own life and that of my father, whose life journey had a significant impact on my own, and explain what I mean when I talk about the 'new Chinese'. In chapter 2, I define the different generations of Chinese migrants who have arrived in Australia since the nineteenth century. In chapter 3, I describe the four generations of Chinese since the establishment of Communist China and introduce more real stories of life since the end of the Cultural Revolution, when China was transformed from a poor and politically rigid country to what it is today. In chapter 4, I try to draw an outline of politics in China—without getting my book banned in my home country. In chapter 5, I talk about traditional Chinese culture and how it continues to shape the mindset of the Chinese today.

In the second half of the book, I touch on some more practical issues relating to the new Chinese. In chapter 6, I look at how the Chinese came to be so rich in just a few decades, and in chapter 7 I discuss how the Chinese spend their money and also offer some pointers on how to sell to the Chinese. In chapter 8, I talk about the Chinese working in Australia and illustrate how different life would have been for them had they been working in China. Here I talk about why I felt I had to 'escape' from China when I did. In the final chapter I offer my views on China's future.

I hope you enjoy reading my story and the story of the new China.

CHAPTER 1

THE NEW CHINESE

MY FATHER'S STORY

In the autumn of 1976, Chairman Mao Zedong passed away. Shortly afterwards the notorious Cultural Revolution, which had ravaged China for a decade, finally ended. Along with the massive damage to the country's economic and social systems, the country's education system was in a shambles. No one went to a real university during that 10-year period because a vast number of university scholars and lecturers were humiliated, persecuted or even killed by the mob. The re-established central government had many competing priorities, but education, a great Chinese tradition that had survived the 10 years of catastrophe, was near the top of the list.

In late 1977, China officially restored its National Higher Education Entrance Examination (Gaokao, equivalent to the HSC in Australia). According to historical data, after the initial screening, about 5.7 million persons took the admission exam, but only 272 971, about 4.8 per cent, were admitted to universities in 1978.

My father was born in 1957 and grew up in a small county called Boli, in the city of Qitaihe in northeast China. He was among the lucky 272 971 intake of new university students. Leaving his hometown, and with great hopes for the future, he went to the country's just-restored engineering school to study coalmine engineering. Four years later, in 1982, he graduated with a bachelor's degree in engineering. In the same year, he married my mother and I was born in Qitaihe.

I am going to say a little more about the city of Qitaihe, to give you a better picture of my hometown. It is a very small city in the province of Heilongjiang with a population of just over 900 000 (based on the 2010 census). In case you don't already know, any city with a population of less than one million people is considered small and insignificant in China. My hometown is almost never mentioned on national news, except when a major mining accident occurs and many people are killed. Even then it is soon forgotten again.

For a long time the city had depended solely on coalmining. My father had worked in a coalmine since he was a teenager, so studying coalmine engineering just made sense. While the admission exam was tough, as the four years' study must have been, 'looking for a job' was not a challenge in China back then. When he graduated and returned to Qitaihe, he was the first person in 10 years to have been to university. So he immediately got his ideal job—a highly valued and respected position as a mining engineer in the city's Mining Bureau. At the same time he married his high-school sweetheart—my mother. So he had a really great start in life and his career.

As young people my parents worked extremely hard. They weren't alone in this—the whole country worked hard. When the 10 years of craziness finally ended, people were thrilled by Deng Xiaoping's 'reforms and opening up' program. Although politics remained a sensitive topic, for the first time since 1949 ordinary people no longer had to worry that their property or even their lives could be taken away based on unpredictable, unaccountable policies and political zealotry. They could now focus on rebuilding their lives through hard work. And they were allowed to own 'more than average' and accumulate personal wealth (a life-threatening risk during the Cultural Revolution). This was a huge change from the distorted 'communist' system and planned economy, which had made everyone's life equally poor and hopeless.

But back to my father's story. While he and my mother had both worked extremely hard, they had absolutely no time for me. I spent my entire childhood with relatives far from home. I was not alone in this. My parents' generation dedicated themselves to making a good living, which didn't leave much time for bringing up kids. This focus gained official support in 1979, when the one-child policy was enforced at the national level.

So my parents could not have had another child even if they had wanted to. They would risk losing their jobs and all their possessions for breaking this law. But, honestly, they probably did not want another child anyway. The country was poor—everyone was poor. The only thing on people's minds then was to grow enough food and to earn enough to escape poverty. Having more kids could only slow them down. Hard work was *everything*—that was the theme of the era.

All this meant that now, as they turn 60, my parents face numerous health problems. My father's years in deep coalmines left him with serious knee damage, forcing him to undergo knee replacement surgery not long ago.

Ironically, once we had enough food, overconsumption of high-calorie food became a new social challenge. When my father was young, there was no such thing as a gym in China. Doing physical exercise routines, even outdoors, would have seemed like an excessive waste of time and money. And people were not conscious of the need to eat healthily and keep fit. Evenings would often be taken up with work-based social engagements with colleagues, clients, suppliers and strategic partners (such as government officials), usually involving a high level of alcohol consumption. My father never drank much, but for many of his generation and after, long-term overconsumption of alcohol has caused many health problems.

I won't say much about smoking and the Chinese cigarette industry, because my father never smoked. But I'll just point out that, for many complex reasons, smoking in public areas, even indoor areas, is still allowed and indeed common in China. You can imagine the health problems the cigarette industry has caused in China over the past 30 years.

Byproducts of rapid economic growth and ballooning energy consumption, air pollution and water contamination are huge problems that will take another 30 years to fix. It is likely that these environmental problems will shorten the lives of many in my parents' generation by at least a few years. All these health threats have helped fuel China's current demand for Australian health products and medical services. An Australian company that bottled and sold fresh air to China made the news last year. And that was not at all funny.

MY STORY

Because of the hard work of my parents' generation, my generation of Chinese, especially those living in the cities and on the east coast, never had to worry about food. My father's generation faced the challenge of malnutrition when they were young; in contrast, my generation faces the problem of childhood obesity.

I was 10 months old when I left my parents to live with relatives. I grew up with *A-po*, my mother's aunt, in the city of Suzhou (population 10 million plus), near Shanghai in eastern China and about 2600 killometres away from Qitaihe. I know it is hard for an Australian to comprehend, but the difference between Qitaihe and Suzhou was massive. Not just the population size or weather or dialect, but *everything*. To put it in simple terms, think of the Great Wall of China, which was built by the Chinese to defend against invasions by nomads from the north. Qitaihe was far beyond the wall, deep in the territory of 'the wildlings'. (If you have watched *Game of Thrones*, you will know what I am talking about.) Suzhou, at the other extreme, was established in 500 BC as the capital of the Wu Kingdom. It was the most educated city in Chinese history. I hope this helps you to imagine the level of bullying I suffered as a fat 'wildling' kid from far 'beyond the wall'.

After 10 years in Suzhou I finally became one of them. I had many friends and spoke both Mandarin (the official Chinese language) and Wu (the Suzhou dialect), the difference between them comparable to that between French and German. Then sadly, for family reasons, I was forced to move back to the northeast to live with my uncle's family.

Arriving from the south with a totally bizarre accent, I had to work very hard to win acceptance by my northern Chinese classmates. Being a 'northerner' by birth did not make it much easier, but after a few years I became one of them again. I have lived in the provinces of Jilin and Liaoning, both bordering North Korea. I've not personally been to North Korea, but many Korean Chinese live in that area.

From the books I have read and the documentaries I have watched, it seems to me that North Korea is probably at the same stage as China was during the Cultural Revolution. I could not imagine myself living in that environment; it was just too hard. From my parents' point of view, I am from the 'spoiled' generation. I did not really feel that when I was a kid, but when I grew up and got to understand how the people of North Korea live today, and what it was like in China before the 1980s, I think my parents were probably right.

Not having to worry about food is only one part of it. When I was a kid we started seeing amazing things entering China, such as Coca-Cola and KFC. We watched Mickey Mouse and *Transformers* and lots of Japanese cartoons. Western movies, such as James Bond, and American drama became popular in China. Everyone at school was learning English (my parents' generation had mainly learned Russian at school), and people started to go overseas to study and do business.

My parents had great career paths in China itself and did not even think about going overseas. They moved from Qitaihe to Harbin, the capital city of Heilongjiang province, then to the national capital, Beijing. In 1997 I moved to Beijing to join them. Again, some of my schoolmates were very mean to kids like me from 'the villages'. I'll talk more about discrimination inside China in the next chapter, but you can probably imagine the attitude of people living in the capital (where the Emperor had lived) towards the rest of the country. I survived high school, and by the time I entered university in 2000 no one could detect my accent and everyone thought that I was an authentic Beijing boy.

My father's Gaokao examination was extremely hard and competitive; mine too was painful, although the success ratio was much better. I obtained a Bachelor of Economics with a major in international economics and trade. My father had decided my major, and it had seemed like a great choice back then. Everyone knew that after years of negotiation China would very soon be entering the World Trade Organization (WTO — China joined in November 2001). It was clear that China would need a lot of talent to manage international trade.

It was only after I graduated that I came to realise that no one really needed a university degree to do international business. Since 1978 literally millions of people in China had been conducting international trade, and millions of people (some of whom did not even speak English or any foreign language) left China to do business. I suppose I could have joined a trading company after I graduated from the country's top business school, but I just hated the fact that there was nothing special about me or the things I had learned.

I decided I was not ready to work yet. I needed to learn something really useful. My parents encouraged me to go overseas to study. Like almost all of the Chinese students you see in

Australia today, I received full support from my parents to study accounting in Australia. To an Australian, studying overseas is a great experience, but to a Chinese back then it meant a lot more than this.

Since the end of the Cultural Revolution the world had started to see international students from China again, but initially all of them were sponsored by the government. They were typically extremely talented and top-ranked students such as Li Cunxin (the author of *Mao's Last Dancer*). Private individuals then could not afford to fund their children to study overseas, especially in developed countries such as the United States or Australia. It was just too expensive for a Chinese family. But since my generation (and probably even a few years before me), Chinese families were able to cover the tuition fees and living expenses in expensive countries such as Australia. This change in itself was groundbreaking.

Education, as I have already noted, has always had a strong tradition among the Chinese people, and they are willing to pay crazy amounts for it. Sending me to Australia to study cost the equivalent of 10 years' salary of an ordinary worker in a typical Chinese city (enough to buy a new property back then), and my parents did not hesitate for a second. They were so excited when I received admission letters from the three top universities in Sydney. They were very proud of me. I was overjoyed, but I also felt the pressure because of my parents' investment and expectations. It was with great anticipation, and total ignorance of what awaited me, that I landed in Australia in 2004 to start my journey in Sydney.

WHY SHOULD AN AUSTRALIAN READ THIS BOOK?

Without great financial pressures, my life in Sydney as a student was relatively easy. I had to do part-time work for experience, but I could also focus on study. I graduated in 2007 and got married in 2009. After a few years of real-world accounting work experience I returned to China in 2010. I imagined returning in glory, just as my father had in 1982. I thought, with my Australian qualification and work experience, I should find a great job and join the country's elite.

I could not have been more naive or wrong. The country I returned to in 2010, only six years after I had left it, was no longer the China I knew. In the intervening years, many thousands of international students had returned and massive development had taken place, even through the global financial crisis (GFC). It didn't seem like the country needed me at all. And honestly, after kicking off my professional experience in Australia, I saw I could never fit into the work environment in China. Over my parents' strong objections, I quickly planned my 'escape' from China and in 2011 Zhen and I came back to Sydney.

Sydney is now my home. In fact, I have lived in this city longer than in any other. Of course, I had to learn real English (as opposed to the Chinese textbook version) and work on my accent again, just as I had done so many times as a kid. I have made many Australian friends, and I feel I am more or less one of them now. Like all the Chinese living in Australia, I learned not only the language, but also the culture, with great difficulty. But I had long ago learned the importance, as a newcomer, of learning about and respecting the local culture and becoming part of it, whether in China or another country.

Until recently, I didn't feel Australians really needed to know much about my language and culture, because it was not really relevant to their lives. But the world is changing much faster than any of us expected. Since I got here, more and more Chinese have arrived, and they have come for a variety of reasons. Many international students like me come here to learn new things. While many of my generation of Chinese students had to take on part-time work to subsidise their tuition fees and living costs, the new generation of students are much wealthier. They work for fun and experience, rather than the money. It is they who have driven the development of new restaurants and rental markets around major campus areas.

Like me, they love Australia and admire the Australian lifestyle, and they want to live here permanently. While it took me years of saving before I could afford my first Australian property, they can buy big houses and apartments while they are still at school because their parents are happy to fund them. In the past few years, Australia has seen a massive rise in real estate investments from China, which has driven up local property prices significantly. When it comes to real estate, it seems like the Chinese are everywhere, and they are loaded with enough cash to buy all of Australia.

With all this going on my Australian friends and clients became curious about what was happening in China. Most of them still imagine a land from the 1970s, a strange and cruel communist country like North Korea, as depicted in the old Chinese books and movies. It sometimes takes great effort to persuade them of how much the country has changed since the Cultural Revolution.

Another significant change from the Australian perspective is the Free Trade Agreement (FTA) signed between China and Australia in 2015. While China is already Australia's largest trading partner, the FTA will no doubt lift this relationship to the next level. Many of my friends in business are seeking opportunities to sell to the Chinese; many more are already doing so. Probably for the first time, they feel the need to learn more about China, its language, its people and its culture.

While they are excited about the trading opportunities, they are puzzled by the way the Chinese do things. For example, in 2016 the level of exports of agricultural products to China was unprecedented. On the negative side, earlier this year Chinese entrepreneurs bought up every jar of baby formula from every supermarket and shipped them to China to sell for a profit. This caused great inconvenience to local mothers (including Chinese mothers) and created a very negative public image of the Chinese.

Then there is the South China Sea arbitration, where it seems like the Chinese are flouting international law by laying claim to a wide scattering of disputed islands, reefs and banks. Every story is complicated. Without a certain level of background knowledge, it is hard to comprehend what the Chinese (both the country and its people) are doing and why. To most Australians, it probably does not matter, but if you feel you are surrounded by Chinese, or your life is impacted by the Chinese in some way, or you seek to profit from trading with China, then building up some knowledge of modern China is essential.

For most people living in Australia, I can assure you that your knowledge about the Chinese (both in Australia and in China) is outdated. I know this because my own knowledge of China and its people was outdated after only a few years of absence. The last time I went to Beijing, while studying at university in Sydney, was in 2007. Just three years later, in 2010, I returned to Beijing, and I could barely even recognise my own neighbourhood.

The scale of change after the 2008 Beijing Olympics was huge. To the best of my recollection, there were two subway lines in Beijing when I left; now there are 18. Before 2010 I had never taken a high-speed train, much to my Chinese friends' amusement. Indeed, returning to the vast cities of Beijing and Shanghai, I suddenly became a 'village boy' again. The number of new buildings, the flood of new cars, luxury goods everywhere — all of this shocked me. And prices had more than tripled in China in just a few years.

When I first came to Australia I was struck by how much everything cost here, but when I returned to China in 2010 I could only think, how has China become so expensive now? What happened while I was away? It took me a few years to understand and accept this change. For the most part, there is a recognition in the western world that China is no longer the poor third-world country it used to be. Fundamental changes have taken place there. In this book I will outline these changes and convey something of their significance, along with useful practical information, to Australian readers.

DEFINING THE NEW CHINESE

You may be wondering why this book is called *The New Chinese*. What is new about these Chinese? What other Chinese are there, and how are they different? This is a complex topic, and here I will try to be as concise as possible. While I certainly don't want to turn this into a history book, I cannot avoid history when talking about China. So I'll briefly touch on some of the essential background information regarding different Chinese people.

More than a hundred years ago, there was pretty much only one Chinese people — those who lived in the Qing empire. The thousands of Chinese villagers drawn by Australia's gold fever came out of the Qing empire. Some few Chinese had arrived in Australia in the British colony's early years, but the first wave of Chinese migrants were attracted by the gold rush around the mid nineteenth century and worked mainly as indentured labourers to escape poverty at home. The descendants of these early settlers have been living in Australia for at least four or five generations.

A few years after this first wave of migrants left home, China was enveloped by revolution. A leading revolutionary, who would become the founding father of the new republic, was Sun Zhongshan, an overseas Chinese educated in Honolulu, Hawaii. Passionate about American-style democracy, Sun devoted many years of struggle to overturning the old Qing empire. He became the first president of the Republic of China in 1912.

In 1919, two years after the Union of Soviet Socialist Republics was established by the Russian Bolsheviks, the Communist Party of China was founded. Between 1927 and 1937, civil war pitted the Nationalists' army against the growing insurgency of the 'Red Army' led by the Communist Party. In 1937 this fratricidal war was put on hold when Japan invaded China.

The country's survival depended on the old adversaries setting aside their differences to defend the nation against the common foe. With some support from the US and the Soviet Union, it took them eight years to drive the Japanese out of China. But peace remained elusive. What became known as the second civil war between the Nationalists and the Communists broke out in 1945. Four years later, in 1949, remnants of the Nationalist forces and government, under the protection of the US Navy, evacuated to the island of Formosa (Taiwan), where they have maintained an alternative government ever since.

The Communists' overwhelming victory was based not only on Soviet support, but more importantly on the support of most of the people in the country. With popular backing, the new China—the People's Republic of China—was established.

Hong Kong and Macau have their own interesting stories. Both cities had been important trading ports since the Ming dynasty (about AD 1500). After the Opium Wars, Hong Kong became a British colony and Macau became a colony of Portugal. Until they were returned to China, in 1997 and 1999 respectively, they had never known Communist rule. Since their return to China they have been accorded unique status as Special Administrative Regions, retaining most elements of their capitalist and western legal systems.

So people who grew up in Taiwan, Hong Kong or Macau never experienced the Cultural Revolution or indeed any of the social instability endured on the mainland in the new China. No doubt they have faced different challenges that drove the development of their own local cultures, but they have also been a part of the wider world for much longer than the new China. For these reasons, they have become very different from mainland Chinese.

So before I start, to avoid any confusion, here are my definitions of the central terms used in these pages. For the purposes of this book, the 'new Chinese' are Chinese people who were born in mainland China after 1949. They grew up in the 'new China', which is the People's Republic of China (PRC), commonly referred to in the western world as 'Communist China'.

I will touch on the Chinese born in Australia because they are still perhaps the most important segment of Australian Chinese society. But again, for the purposes of this book, they are not the 'new Chinese', because they grew up in Australia. Although they may have been influenced by their parents' culture, that culture will have been significantly different from the 'new Chinese' culture we will talk about in this book.

The new Chinese do not include anyone who was born and raised in Hong Kong, Macau or Taiwan either. They may look Chinese and are arguably of Chinese origin (the official Chinese position is that Taiwan is part of China, though some of my Taiwanese friends would disagree), but they were born and raised in a quite different social environment, and are therefore very different from the new Chinese that are my main subject.

Neither will this book examine Singaporean Chinese or Malaysian Chinese or Chinese Americans, all of whom again have different stories that I know little about. Maybe in the future I will get to talk to them, and even live in their countries to gain a better understanding, but for now I will focus on the 1.3 billion–plus mainland Chinese, and especially those who have travelled from there to Australia.

Besides telling my own story, I will interview a range of people who were born in the new China at different times and came to Australia for different reasons. I hope these stories will help you to better understand China and its new generation.

CHAPTER SUMMARY

- After the Cultural Revolution and Deng Xiaoping's reforms, the vast majority of the country embraced hard work to escape poverty and rebuild their lives.

- One consequence of this single-minded focus was that they had little time for children, and the one-child policy was their ally in this.

- Education has a strong tradition in China. When the Cultural Revolution ended, so too did the suppression of the universities and of education. Parents were (and are) prepared to pay vast amounts for their children's studies.

- With the large numbers of new Chinese coming to study and work in Australia, and closer trade relations between our two countries, it is more important than ever for Australians to learn about their Chinese neighbours and those they would do business with.

- For the purposes of this book, the 'new Chinese' are those who were born in mainland China after 1949 and who grew up in the People's Republic of China (PRC)—the 'new China'.

AUSTRALIA
27 FEB 2012
IMMIGRATION
SYDNEY
AIRPORT

CHAPTER 2

FROM THE GOLD RUSH TO THE PROPERTY RUSH

CANTONESE SPEAKERS

When I first arrived in Australia at the end of 2004 there were already many Chinese living here; most of them, though, are quite different from the new Chinese. First, the majority are Cantonese speakers (if they still speak Chinese at home). They are descendants of the earliest wave of Chinese migrants bound for the goldfields. According to historical records, about 11 500 Chinese from the old Qing empire arrived in Australia in 1855 as contract labourers. By the 1860s the number of Chinese in Australia stood at around 40 000. Most spoke Cantonese and came from the Guangdong province in southern China.

Today, as someone from the mainland who speaks only Mandarin, I would find it very hard to land a part-time job in a Sydney Chinese restaurant, even as a dishwasher, because most restaurants serve Cantonese food, catering mainly to local

Australians and Cantonese-speaking Chinese. Speaking Cantonese is one of the job requirements. Poor overseas students like me from mainland China sometimes feel discriminated against not so much by white Australians as by the Cantonese speakers who settled in Australia much earlier.

It may surprise Australian readers, but among Chinese people the language you speak and understand makes a lot of difference. When first meeting a Chinese person in Australia, you really need to know whether he or she speaks Cantonese or Mandarin. To complicate matters further, there are literally hundreds of different dialects in China spoken by people from different provinces and cities. To keep things simple, I will talk only about Cantonese speakers, Mandarin speakers and, to a lesser extent, Shanghainese speakers.

When I grew up in China, Cantonese was viewed as a very fancy language, not in the sense that it sounded beautiful, like French, but in the sense that people had the general perception that Cantonese speakers were richer compared with the vast majority of the people, who were Mandarin speakers.

Cantonese is a language spoken in the Guangdong (Canton) province in southern China. The capital city of the province is Guangzhou, one of the earliest trading ports established in China. Besides Guangzhou, there are three other very special cities in the area—Hong Kong, Macau and Shenzhen. As I've noted, Hong Kong and Macau were for many years European colonies, and remain today a part of the developed world with a per capita GDP hundreds of times greater than in mainland China.

Shenzhen was developed as the first 'experimental' city when Communist China decided to open up its borders to international business again, simply because it was geographically close to Hong Kong. Most industries in Hong Kong had moved to Guangdong province during the 1980s and 1990s to make space for Hong Kong's growing service and finance industries.

Led by Shenzhen, Guangdong was the first province in China to benefit from the new policies of Deng Xiaoping, and it became the richest province in China during the 1990s. Millions of Chinese from the poorer provinces, especially rural areas, moved to Guangdong province to look for work. These very diligent people comprised the cheap labour force that fuelled China's magical economic growth over the past 30 years.

It should not surprise you that some of the rich Cantonese speakers looked down on some of the poor Mandarin speakers (or those who did not even speak Mandarin, but only the dialect of their hometown) who had migrated to Guangdong province to make a living. Putting the prejudice issue aside, Chinese people in general think highly of Cantonese speakers, not only because of their wealth, but also because of their entrepreneurial and adventurous minds.

Compared with people from some other provinces in China, Cantonese-speaking people are more willing to leave their hometowns and go to foreign countries to look for opportunities. The earliest Chinese settlers in any western country, including Australia, were probably from Guangdong. So they started to settle in Australia at least a hundred years earlier than the Chinese from other provinces did.

The other wave of Cantonese-speaking Chinese to Australia came from the city of Hong Kong before 1997. There were many suspicions and concerns in the lead-up to the transfer of Hong Kong back to China in 1997. Many Hong Kong residents chose to migrate to 'safer' western countries. Their concerns were legitimate back then. 'Capitalism vs communism' is another common fault line of prejudice among Chinese. It took me a few years to understand the history behind this bias.

Many more of my generation and those who have arrived since, who came to Australia as international students or as skilled migrants, spoke both Cantonese and Mandarin. Unlike early settlers and Hong Kong Chinese, they were born in the new China, and, even if they spoke Cantonese at home, they were educated in Mandarin at school, so they speak both languages fluently.

To get a better understanding of their thinking, I interviewed Joey, who was born in 1993 and is a current UNSW student. I asked her whether, as someone from Guangdong province who speaks both languages, she felt different from other mainlanders. She did feel different, she admitted, but not too much. Culturally, she felt closer to Mandarin speakers than to someone from Hong Kong who spoke Cantonese. Although they shared the same language, it sometimes felt like people from Hong Kong looked at her differently.

Part of this distance from people outside Guangdong might be explained by different media influences. Joey rarely watches CCTV News (which is in Mandarin) and more often tunes in to TVB (a Cantonese channel broadcast from Hong Kong). When it comes to social media, though, she favours WeChat, which aligns her with the mainland Chinese, as people outside China and those who do not connect to the Chinese mindset rarely use WeChat.

WeChat and Weibo are the only major social media platforms that can be easily accessed nationwide in China. From observation I have found that Cantonese speakers from Hong Kong or overseas rarely use WeChat, preferring Facebook and WhatsApp. In Australia Joey mostly hangs out with friends from mainland China and only speaks Mandarin, but speaking both languages is still an advantage, especially when ordering dishes in a Cantonese-style restaurant!

Another source of pride for Cantonese speakers, apart from their unparalleled economic advantage until the mid 1990s, was popular culture in Cantonese. Since 1980 many Cantonese songs, movies and TV shows entered mainland China from Hong Kong. Famous Chinese movie stars such as Bruce Lee and Jackie Chan came from Hong Kong and initially spoke only Cantonese.

A passion for the popular culture they represented encouraged the rest of the country to learn Cantonese. In those days some famous singers from mainland China had to learn to sing in

Cantonese simply because the market for Cantonese popular songs was bigger than that for Mandarin songs until the late 1990s. Although Mandarin has been the official Chinese language since the Qing dynasty, it did not appear as important as Cantonese until very recently.

Many Chinese-language books teach Cantonese pronunciation rather than Mandarin even today. It is definitely a language worth learning, but if an Australian friend asks me now which of the two to learn, I advise Mandarin. This is simply because the Mandarin-speaking population is far bigger, and the economic advantage of the Cantonese-speaking population has been gradually reduced with the rise of other cities and provinces whose common tongue is Mandarin.

MANDARIN SPEAKERS

In this chapter, when I speak of Mandarin speakers, I'm referring to Mandarin speakers from mainland China. There are other Mandarin speakers, of course. People of Chinese origin from Taiwan and Singapore also speak Mandarin, but, as I have noted, they are not the new Chinese I am describing in this book. Generally, Mandarin speakers arrived in Australia a lot later, and since the Cultural Revolution most came from mainland China. Here I am going to use Mandarin speakers and mainland Chinese interchangeably, and I will explain why soon.

First, let's look at the Mandarin language. Mandarin is regarded as official or standard Chinese — it's called *Putonghua* in Chinese, which literally means the 'common tongue'. Before I came to Australia I didn't know what the word 'Mandarin' meant or why the official Chinese is called 'Mandarin', so I searched for an answer.

One of the stories about the origin of the name actually makes sense. *Man Da Ren* was the name for a government official in the Qing dynasty. The Qing dynasty was established by the nomadic Manchu people who lived beyond the Great Wall in northeast

China. Now defined as an ethnic minority Chinese group, a few hundred years ago they were not even recognised as Chinese by the majority Han people. The Manchus conquered the whole of China, but to rule the country they had to learn the Han Chinese language and culture.

The Manchu language, both spoken and written, was completely different from the Han Chinese language, which must have taken the Manchus a great deal of effort to learn. Their pronunciation was different from that of the Han. Since they could not manage the five or seven tones found in the other Chinese dialects, especially those in the south, Mandarin uses only four tones. In time the Manchus established their language as the official Chinese spoken in the country's capital, Beijing.

Now to the crux of the story. When western missionaries visited China during the Qing dynasty, they needed to deal with government officials, who were mostly Manchu people. They politely addressed the officials as *Man Da Ren* (meaning 'Your Excellency from Manchu'), which created the word 'Mandarin' to represent the Chinese spoken by officials.

After the Qing dynasty, both the Republic of China and the People's Republic of China made Mandarin the official Chinese language. This means every child in mainland China will learn Mandarin at school. In 2010 there were about 960 million native Mandarin speakers in the world. By comparison, there are only 60 million native Cantonese speakers and 365 million native English speakers in the world. These population figures alone make Mandarin a very important spoken language.

Outside China, more and more people, including Cantonese speakers, are learning Mandarin. The Mandarin speakers now arriving in Australia will not feel the same as I did a decade ago. I know a few Australian friends who have learned Mandarin and speak it perfectly. I find it is so cool for a westerner to speak fluent Chinese. Chinese people just adore them.

One great example is the former prime minister of Australia Kevin Rudd, who speaks perfect Mandarin. He did not have any particular leaning towards China or Chinese migrants in terms of political policy, but so many Chinese just love him. I guess speaking someone's language does say a lot about the person's interest in and understanding of that language and culture.

Let's take a look at the comparative numbers of Mandarin versus Cantonese speakers in Australia. Based on the 2001 census, some 244000 Australians spoke Cantonese at home, compared with about 220000 who spoke Mandarin. A decade later, in the 2011 census, the numbers had risen to 263000 Cantonese speakers and 336000 Mandarin speakers. In a decade, while the Cantonese speakers increased by 19000, Mandarin speakers increased by 116000.

In addition, given that many of these Cantonese-speaking families settled in Australia long ago, their children probably speak more English than Cantonese. It is clear that Mandarin is now used more commonly in Australia than Cantonese. This is also evidenced by the growing number of Chinese restaurants in Australia that feature Sichuan cuisine, which is too spicy for most Cantonese-speaking Chinese.

Breaking down Mandarin speakers by province would take forever—I could write a separate book on just that. It is as difficult for a native Australian to distinguish a Mandarin speaker from one province of China or another as it is for me to tell the difference between a red wine from one region or another. But unless your ambition is to become a sommelier of languages, that knowledge probably will not be necessary.

So I am going to discuss the differences between various Mandarin speakers only on a general, large-category level. For example, we can divide them into northerners and southerners. Broadly speaking, northerners are more uninhibited and less calculating. Southerners are gentler and better educated, perhaps more business-minded too. This kind of generalisation does not hold up when we compare people from province to province or city to city, let alone on an individual basis.

The few major cities that do not speak Cantonese have shown very different characteristics based on their own particular history and culture. Beijing, for example, as the nation's capital, was the home of Mandarin. Native residents of Beijing often do not hide their pride in being citizens of the capital. They tend to be more politically aware and opinionated.

Going south, in the famous city of Shanghai most people speak Shanghainese at home and Mandarin at work or school. According to many of my friends who lived there, Shanghainese people, especially the older generation, often despise people who do not speak Shanghainese (a trait they share with some Cantonese speakers). Living in the most developed city in the Far East with a glorious history, they have every reason to be proud.

Interestingly, as more and more outsiders have migrated to and adopted these cities over the past 30 years, the traditionally distinct Beijing and Shanghai cultures have morphed into a more generalised mainland Chinese culture. This has certainly made dealing with people and doing business in mainland China a lot easier.

One common misconception in Australia is that all Chinese from mainland ('Communist') China are communists with aggressive political views. This could not be further from the truth. As I discuss in the next chapter, many of the younger generation have zero knowledge of or interest in political matters in China. Some who came from mainland China in earlier times suffered tragically in China for political reasons and understandably had strong antipathy towards the power structure in China.

For example, a great number of Chinese in their mid forties today settled in Australia after being granted political asylum by the Bob Hawke government in the late 1980s. As a result of their personal experience with the Chinese government and their personal choices, these Chinese migrants are likely to have very different political views from the generation that came after them.

Learning that someone is 'a Mandarin speaker', therefore, will not tell you much about the person you are talking to. A better question to ask when you meet a new friend from China is probably, 'Where in China have you come from?' What you can derive from this is still quite limited, but in combination with the person's age group, you should get a sense of his or her background and what you might expect from the conversation.

RICH CHINESE

There are rich Chinese in every province and every city in China, including the poorest, so it is impossible to assess people's personal wealth from their origin. As we have noted, Cantonese speakers are generally no longer richer than Mandarin speakers. But although generalisation and profiling are wrong in principle, they do offer interesting insights. And more often than not they will throw up meaningful information to get a conversation started.

Let me give you one simple example. As a CPA mentor, I talk to young accounting students all the time. One day a girl from China came to speak to me after a presentation. She was an accounting student from the University of Sydney, about 19 years old. She asked me if I did any business outside work, then she asked me to comment on her idea of establishing an online learning platform for overseas students. I listened to her business plan, and I thought the idea was great. I talked about the Business Model Canvas, the Lean Startup method and so on, just as you would see in any modern-day startup textbook. Then I asked how much money she was planning to invest. She gave me a figure that surprised me. She said she planned to invest $100 000–$150 000.

I said that was quite a large sum. (I assumed all her money was from her parents, as is the case for most Chinese students here.) I asked if her parents were aware of her plans and would they support her on this? She said they would, as both her parents were in business. I could not tell from her accent which city she was from (unlike their parents, the younger generation rarely reveal a strong accent when speaking Mandarin). So I asked her, 'Do you mind telling me which city you are from?' She said, 'My home is in Wenzhou.' At that the whole conversation immediately made sense to me.

Wenzhou, in Zhejiang province, is probably the most entrepreneurial and adventurous city in the whole of China. The city has a vast number of small manufacturing businesses, almost all of them privately owned, that make almost every domestic product you can find in the world with the 'Made in China' tag. These business owners have accumulated huge wealth as a result of decades of business ventures and hard work.

The whole country admires the entrepreneurial spirit of the Wenzhou people. When we discover someone is from Wenzhou, we automatically assume that his or her family has billions of yuan (Chinese currency), although we can sometimes be wrong. I once talked to a Wenzhou friend who was asking my advice on whether to stay in Australia after graduation from UNSW. She said her family, although from Wenzhou, was not very rich. Of course, I did not take this comment at face value, because I knew there are almost no poor (by normal definition) people in that city.

I suggested that as her 'not very rich' family doubtless were worth more than 100 million yuan, she should probably go back home rather than stay in Australia. She said they had only 80 million in assets (about $16 million), which was not quite enough for the whole family. Her reply left me speechless, but it also reinforced my belief that everyone from Wenzhou was rich.

Although the people from Wenzhou have plenty of money, no one dislikes them for it, because we know they have made their money through hard work (at least most of them), and they are willing to take high risks for high returns. People from this city don't have to learn any foreign languages before they travel the world to do international trade (something I spent four years in my country's top business school doing). They just do it, and do pretty well.

My mother once told me that, back in the 1970s, when northeast China was the most developed region in China, many people from Wenzhou went up there to take on the hard labouring work (such as cleaning rubbish) that the locals did not want to do. Wenzhou people never hesitate to go anywhere in China or overseas, as long as there is money to be made. One of China's most successful businessmen, Jack Ma, founder of Alibaba, is from Zhejiang province. Since 1995 he has invested all his savings and devoted his whole life to building the online B2B and B2C platform in China.

When he started, most Chinese did not even know the internet existed. It was that kind of vision, courage and persistence that have made Jack Ma, and like-minded entrepreneurs from Zhejiang province, so successful. They are not only financially rich; they are rich in their thinking and in their willingness to act. This mindset and readiness to act is not commonly seen in other cities and provinces.

Wenzhou is a very special case. Outside this city, rich Chinese can be found everywhere in China, but more often on the east coast and in the cities. Because of its geographical importance, population density and access to major infrastructure and logistics facilities, the east coast has hundreds of thousands of factories and other wealth-creating businesses.

The inland and western areas of China remained largely undeveloped until the past decade. The central government's strategic policy to develop the west worked in some places, and certainly made some people rich, but it did not benefit enough of the population. People living in the west and in rural areas in the east were forced to go to the major cities to make a living.

Demographically, urbanisation has been the dominant theme across the country over the past decades, and it still is. The cities are becoming bigger day by day. The population of Beijing stood at 11.5 million in 2000; it was 21.7 million in 2015. The population of Shanghai was 16.7 million in 2000; it reached 24.1 million in 2015. These increases are partly explained by organic growth, but are mainly due to people from other parts of the country migrating to the cities for economic reasons.

The increases in population and income have sent property prices through the roof in these major cities, with the average price per square metre more than tripling in the past decade. A small three-bedroom apartment in Beijing today would cost over $1 million. Most people believe that those who own a property in Beijing or Shanghai *are* the rich Chinese. A lot of the older Chinese who have worked all their lives are expected to have more than one property. The increase in property prices alone has created millions of rich Chinese in the major cities. To these people, purchasing another property in Sydney or Brisbane for investment or holiday is as easy as pie.

POOR CHINESE

'Rich' and 'poor' are relative terms, of course. Australians are unlikely to meet Chinese people who are living below the poverty threshold. Such people do not have enough money to travel here for a holiday or to study, and they certainly do not have the money to invest in Australian property. In this sense, all the Chinese people you meet in Australia are rich.

Even if we set aside the new Chinese for a moment and talk only of the local Chinese who have been here for generations, I am pretty certain they will be considered rich when compared with the average Chinese in China. When I was growing up in China, anyone who had an overseas relative was considered rich. Back then, a great many Chinese workers went to the US or Australia to take on a part-time job in a restaurant, say, and the money they sent back to China was enough to feed their whole family.

During the early 1990s there was a famous novel and soap opera in China called *Beijinger in New York*. From that story, every Chinese came to believe that migrating to a developed country such as the US or Australia was the solution to all of life's problems. Of course, many people seized the opportunity if it arose. There could only be two reasons for not taking that option: either they had better things to do in China or, for economic or other reasons, they found it difficult to make the move. Migrating to Australia is still a popular ambition today, but for quite different reasons. Many Chinese can earn a better income in China than in Australia. They come here for a fairer social environment and cleaner air.

As I have explained, following a few years of studies and work I returned to China in 2010. After the GFC, China was the only major economy in the world that was still booming. My action illustrated what was then a fairly new phenomenon. Before 1990, Chinese migrants to Australia rarely returned to China. Since the mid 1990s, and all the way to my generation, more and more Chinese student graduates and skilled migrants have returned to China to pursue career opportunities.

Between 2000 and 2010, China was absolutely booming. Its GDP grew from just over US$1 trillion to almost US$6 trillion in 2010 (and over US$10 trillion in 2016). Taking out the foreign exchange rate impact, it was still a significant growth over just one decade. By comparison, another super-engine in Asia, India, had a GDP of only US$1.7 trillion in 2010. By just looking at these figures, you can see the scale of growth my peers who did not leave China experienced and the amount of money they made. I actually felt pretty left out in 2010.

So I decided to return to China with all my newly gained knowledge and experience from Australia. I imagined myself getting an awesome job and quickly becoming rich. What absolutely shocked me there was that, unlike the generations of overseas Chinese before me, I was absolutely a 'poor Chinese' when I returned from Australia.

I could not believe the price of basic things. The officially published consumer price index (CPI) increases of between 2 and 6 per cent per annum from 2000 to 2010 was absolute nonsense in a big city such as Beijing. Everything had increased three to five times in price, some things over 10 times. I suddenly realised that I had not updated my price list for China for too many years. I never felt so poor in my life. This, combined with a few other factors, made me decide to return to my normal middle-class life in Australia in 2011. I am not rich by Australian standards, but at least I can afford to support my own family and maintain a comfortable standard of living. It is a lot harder in Beijing.

Most of the new Chinese living in Australia are ordinary Chinese like me. To get educated and prepared for the local job market we spend quite a lot of money here (although it may not seem so much for some of the younger generation whose parents are wealthy). We find a professional job and make an average income. Although China remains a poor country by per capita GDP, quite a few of my friends back there are earning 10 to 20 times what I am as a result of the economic boom. To them, my family's earlier investment on my education seems to have been totally wasted.

But like most Chinese migrants living in Australia, I did not really much care about their view—until recently when I needed to buy a new house for my growing family.

Earlier this year I went to an auction in North Ryde, New South Wales. It is a typical middle-class suburb, and there was nothing really special about the house we wanted to buy. The property was advertised for $1.2 to $1.4 million (it was probably worth $800 000 four years ago). I knew it was going to be a tough one because of the number of Chinese buyers I'd seen at the inspections, but I thought I was fully prepared for the battle.

Once the auction got going it took no more than five minutes to top $1.4 million. From $1.4 to $1.5 million, there were two Chinese families competing, and I still had not said a word. At $1.5 million, when one of the families quit the auction, I started to bid. While I was increasing the bid by one thousand each time, the other family was raising it by ten thousand. I could see they were trying very hard to leave me behind; I was just not sure how far they would go. At $1.6 million I decided to leave the game and let them have the property.

Experiences like that make me feel poor. They also make me realise the unfairness. Plenty of parents in China would fund their children in Australia for the deposit or even the entire cost of the property from their own savings. At that auction, I was competing not with just another local family, but with their entire family, who had a lifetime of savings in their pocket boosted by the economic boom.

Had it been just one young couple bidding against another young couple, I would not have lost that auction. Both my wife and I work full time as professional accountants. We are a typical middle-class family in Sydney, yet we cannot afford a very ordinary house in a very middle-class suburb. I could not afford China in 2010 and came back, but the Chinese inflation had followed me back to Australia and made owning a house completely unaffordable.

I should probably blame the government for poor urban development planning and letting unregulated foreign money in and not doing enough to address affordability issues for the locals. However, because I know the Chinese so well and I am Chinese myself, I have the liberty to blame the cash-loaded Chinese buyers for making me a poor Chinese Australian who cannot afford the perfect house for my children to grow up in. My frustration is shared by many of my friends living in Sydney.

CHAPTER SUMMARY

- The first wave of Chinese migrants to Australia were mostly Cantonese speakers from Guangdong province in southern China drawn by the mid-nineteenth-century gold rushes.

- Mandarin is regarded as official or standard Chinese and is the language in which every child in China is taught at school. There are now some 1 billion native Mandarin speakers in the world (compared with about 60 million native Cantonese speakers).

- Wealth inequality in China is widening.
  Fault lines are forming between the cities that offer work and the emptying villages, and between the booming, urbanised east coast and the underdeveloped rural areas in the west.

- All Chinese migrants to Australia are (relatively speaking) rich, as the poor generally lack the means to travel to or study in Australia.

- Before the 1990s, migrants rarely returned to China; since the mid 1990s growing numbers of student graduates and skilled migrants have returned to China to pursue career opportunities.

CHAPTER 3

FOUR GENERATIONS OF CHANGE

THE 80-HOU

Life is a uniquely personal experience. Every individual lives a different life and has a unique set of experiences that make up his or her memories and shape his or her beliefs. At the same time, people of similar age who come from the same country usually have many experiences in common. These common experiences help shape their common beliefs, which can help us to better understand the generation they represent.

I will start with myself as an example. I am a typical '80-hou' (*hou* means 'after' in Chinese), which is a post-1980 equivalent of the first half of Generation Y in the western world—someone who was born between 1980 and 1989 in the new China. My generation grew up in a rapidly changing environment. My earliest memories are from when I was about five years old.

I lived in the city of Suzhou, together with my mother's aunt, whom I called *A-Po* (local dialect for grandmother), though she was not related to me by blood. We lived together with my cousin, who was the daughter of my grandma's adopted daughter. Back then she was probably 15 or 16.

I remember the three of us lived in a 10-square-metre room and slept in one big wooden bed. Apart from the bed, I cannot remember much other furniture. We had no kitchen and no toilet. It was a small room within a big courtyard, which used to belong to a local big noble family. In 1949 it was confiscated by the Communist government and was divided among many poor residents in the city. Before 1949 it was for one big family; after 1949 that courtyard housed about 10 families—more than 30 people, including children.

There was no running water, just a well near the courtyard entrance. I remember that well vividly because I used to play around it, staring into it and wondering what would happen if I fell in. There were no child protection fences back then. All the water we used—for cooking, bathing and washing clothes—came from that well. Cooking was done on a *yoentan* stove, which was a honeycomb-shaped coal stove. Every day at lunchtime and dinnertime, when every family fired up their coal stoves for cooking, we could see the smoke rising towards the sky from every residence in the city.

We did have an electrical connection at that time, but it was only for lighting. No one we knew could afford whitegoods, nor were any such appliances available for purchase by ordinary people. These goods came in through special channels for special people.

I remember one of the families in the courtyard had a very old black-and-white television. Every night they would set up a table and move their TV to the centre of the courtyard, and all the neighbours would gather around it. Everyone brought their own chairs and watched the TV together and talked about their day's events. There was only one TV channel back then, China Central Television (CCTV). Watching *CCTV News* was important to every Chinese family. They needed to know what new political movements were arising and of any new policies that might promise better living conditions.

I remember watching some of the news. I also remember watching Mickey Mouse on Sunday evenings. That show, broadcast for one hour on Sunday evenings, was the only cartoon show available when I was five or six years old. When I was about seven years old, my grandma barred me from watching TV, because Mickey Mouse was not available and also because there were some very disturbing scenes from Tiananmen Square in Beijing. I really don't remember much except that my older sister (my 'cousin' really, but I call her my sister, in the way my one-child generation often do), who was in the university back then, and her friends were excited and then depressed for a while. No one ever talked about that event again. I had absolutely no idea what had happened.

Soon after 1989 some things seemed to get better inside China. The government decided to knock down the old courtyard to widen the city's major road, and every family was offered a new modern unit. Destroying a 100-year-old heritage house might not sound like a good thing to do today, but 20 years ago everyone welcomed the decision once they were promised a new place with a kitchen and a toilet, and with more room for their growing families. Beginning in the early 1990s, a large number of new high-rise buildings went up in Suzhou and every major city in China. These new buildings created many job opportunities and new homes for the booming population.

My grandma did not move into one of those new buildings. She wanted me to stay in the same school in the city centre, which happened to be the best primary school in Suzhou. For this reason, she traded her new unit with the old courtyard place of another family. It was very similar to our old one. The only difference was that the new place was bigger, with two separate rooms, and running water. Still no toilet, but then running water was a better option, because it meant Grandma no longer had to fetch water from the well.

I remember in 1990, when I was eight years old, turning on the tap and watching with amazement as water flowed out. When my mother came down from the northeast to visit me, she brought a colour TV. That was the year I discovered that Mickey Mouse was actually in colour. I remember watching the 1990 Beijing Asian Games opening ceremony. It was the very first time that Beijing hosted a major international event.

It was on that television, too, that I first heard the names of many countries outside China. I learned that the United States was the most powerful country in the world; that in the Gulf War the US saved Kuwait from the Iraqi invasion using MIM-104 Patriot missiles; that Japan, now China's important trading partner and neighbour, had suffered a great loss during World War II.

Every Chinese kid liked American and Japanese cartoon shows, while the adults enjoyed Fred Dryer and Ken Takakura. In 1991 I heard in the news that the Soviet Union no longer existed. You might have thought it would be shocking news in a communist country such as China, but the impact on people my age was absolutely nil. By 1991 it was clear that China was no longer an ally of the USSR and was far keener to play with the capitalist countries.

Towards the end of my primary schooling I moved back to northeast China, which was then the country's most developed industrial zone. In the city, more and more people left the slums and moved into high-rise units. Living with my uncle, we had running water and even plumbed toilets. I remember the fun of flushing toilets when I was 12. It was as amazing to me as turning on a tap. But even more amazing things were happening. Unattainable luxury goods just a couple of years before, the television, fridge and washing machine, now all had a place in our home.

I touched a computer for the first time in 1993 on a holiday visit to my father, who had one at home. It was an IBM 80386 model. Playing *Snake* on a tiny black screen felt like more fun than any flashy online game today. China may have been over a hundred years behind the US in residential plumbing, but it was only a few years behind in computers, and it was catching up fast. When I went to university, at age 19, most of my classmates had the latest Pentium computer or even a laptop. Most had mobile phones too. It might not sound like a big deal to a western reader but, considering where I had started, these were very big changes.

THE 90-HOU

I could go on and on with my own story, but that is not where I want to go. This personal aside was only to illustrate the scale and speed of changes my generation experienced. It was quite different for the later Chinese Generation Y, which we call the '90-hou' (post-1990) — that is, the generation of Chinese born in the 1990s. Generally, this generation was born and raised in much better material circumstances than my generation.

I interviewed Joyce, who was born in 1993, to learn about her life experiences. Joyce was born into a rural family in the south of China. When she was little, her parents were busy with their new family business. They also wanted her to grow up in a better environment than they could offer. So, like my parents, they took a course that was common back then but would be deemed almost unthinkable today. Since kindergarten she lived at a homestay in the city. Her parents paid the kindergarten supervisor, then her primary school teachers, for her to live with them in the city. She went home only occasionally.

She said she hated the experience, especially in 1999 when her younger sister was born. Unlike Joyce, who had spent her entire childhood with totally unrelated people, her sister grew up at home with her parents. When she was older, however, she came to understand her parents' reasons for doing this. Kids who grew up in the city did get a better education and had a wider vision than village kids. And for this reason, her parents had been willing to spend a lot more money on her upbringing and had sacrificed all that family time.

You might be wondering why she had a sister in 1999, when China was still enforcing the one-child policy. This was actually quite common in southern China, especially in rural areas, where the local government tended to be more 'humane' when executing central government policies. This is because in the rural areas people needed sons. So if their first-born was a girl, a couple would be given a second chance. 'Unfortunately' for Joyce's family, they had a girl both times.

Joyce believed her family treated her like the 'boy' of the family. The great hope they had set on her future made her life experience quite different from that of her younger sister. Joyce recalls an environment while she was growing up that was quite different from mine. She had enjoyed not only running water and a toilet in the unit, but all the electronics you could find in a modern home. Even when she was a young kid, her family had a car. She grew up with KFC, Doraemon (Japanese animation) and American movies.

Her paid guardians did not love her as her parents did, but they did a reasonable job of raising her. When she finished high school she went to the Chinese campus of the University of Nottingham (there were no such institutions when I graduated from high school). Although this university was located in China, she received the same education, all in English, as she would have in England. And it included six months of studies in the UK. Together with her master's degree in Australia, her family must have spent about 800 000 yuan (about $145 000) on her tertiary education. And like my parents, her parents did not hesitate for a moment.

When I asked about her experience in this country, she did not feel Australia to be expensive. One reason for this was that her mental price list for China was updated to 2014 (mine had been locked on 2004, the year I left China); another reason was that she had lived in the UK for six months and had got used to prices in the English-speaking world. This is another big difference between her generation and mine. I had never been anywhere outside China before I came here, because any overseas trip was considered a luxury in my time. In Joyce's experience, travelling outside China was something every middle-class family did during summer and winter vacations.

When I asked her why she chose to study in Australia, she said she had had some bad experiences in the UK. One negative was the weather. For someone coming from southern China, the English weather could be unbearable, and Sydney would be a much better option. Another was that she had felt discriminated against and unwelcome in the UK. One day she was on a bus. A local white kid saw her sitting by the window, and spat on the window to intimidate her then told her to go back to her own country.

It could have been an isolated incident, but in the same circumstances I might well have made the same choice as her. I asked her if she had experienced anything similar while in Sydney. She recalled that once when she went to the Mardi Gras a few drunken people had been quite mean to her and a group of Chinese friends, but she had never had a bad experience with any sober Australians. Overall, she felt she was respected and treated as an equal in Australia.

When I asked Joyce about the Cultural Revolution and the events of 1989, as I expected, she knew pretty much nothing. She certainly had no idea about Tibet or the tensions in the South China Sea. Sometimes ignorance is a blessing. Asked about the current political situation in China, she had no idea at all. She said her generation had absolutely no interest in politics. She read more Australian news than Chinese news. She was not interested in elections or political movements, which might not have existed as far as she was concerned. When I asked about Xi Jinping and his anti-corruption campaign, she said she thought it was pretty cool, but made no further comment. This is quite normal and to be expected from her generation.

Asked about her plans after finishing her degree here, she was certain she would return to China. This is very different from my generation and the generations before me. The new generation of Chinese are much wealthier in China and have a lot more choices than we had. Nor do they have any political reasons to leave China (or to not be allowed to return).

CHINESE GEN X

The parents of the 90-hou were from the generation of Chinese born between 1966 and 1979 in mainland China. I will call them the Chinese Gen X. This generation were born in the period of the Cultural Revolution. It was a difficult time for all Chinese, as pretty much all westerners already know, so I will not go into those stories here. What I will focus on instead is the experience of this generation when growing up in China, especially after the Cultural Revolution.

Let us imagine a boy born in 1966. By the time he became a teenager, Chairman Mao had died and the horrible Cultural Revolution had ended, so he had the opportunity to get a proper education and to go to university—if he lived in the city and studied hard enough. He could even go on to complete his advanced professional education in his twenties. Furthermore, China had opened its borders and international travel had become possible.

Cunxin Li, author of *Mao's Last Dancer*, born in 1961, probably belonged to the last generation of Chinese who really had to defect from China to find a better life elsewhere. I expect many will disagree with this statement; there have been a few other political events since the Cultural Revolution that could have driven people with different political views out of China. In my view, however, it was a combination of dissatisfaction with the country and personal choice that drove these people away. We will talk about this in more detail later.

The Chinese Gen X grew up in a relatively difficult environment, but they also had options that my father's generation never had in their twenties and thirties. To understand their story better, I interviewed my friend C, who was born in 1972. Like me, he calls Sydney home, having lived here for 14 years. He works for a multinational corporation in Sydney for business development with China. Because of the sensitive nature of some of our discussions, he has chosen to remain anonymous in this book.

C, about ten years older than me, was born and grew up in the city of Tianjin, a major trading port with a long history. In Chinese, Tianjin means 'port of the emperor' because it was less than 150 kilometres from the country's capital, Beijing, where the emperor lived. Unlike in my father's day, when less than 5 per cent of applicants were accepted for university, by 1991 there were already hundreds of higher educational institutes in China. So it was relatively easy for C, or any high-school graduate from a large city, to get into a university.

Things were different after they graduated from university, too. When my father graduated, he did not have the option of looking for a job himself but had to go wherever the state appointed him. But for C's generation, the 'double direction option' was available. This simply meant that an employer could choose a graduate but a graduate could also choose an employer. This is the norm these days in China, as it is everywhere else in the world, but back then it was a new phenomenon.

About half of the graduates would go and look for jobs themselves, mainly targeting foreign companies operating in China. In the early 1990s those foreign companies were the most prestigious and high paying. Graduates who got a job in those companies were greatly envied by their peers. This remained the case for the 10 to 15 years that followed. But for personal reasons, C did not choose to work for a foreign company. He decided instead to work in a state-owned trading company in Tianjin.

Back in the early 1990s almost all Chinese trading companies were state owned, because individuals could not afford to set up a trading company. C worked in a few companies and then in a few banks in China. In 2000, inspired by a friend, he applied for a General Skilled Migration visa and moved to Sydney. He had applied to both Australia and Canada, and he was accepted by both countries, but he chose Australia. He found his first local job only a few months after relocating to Sydney.

As a professional, he moved from job to job and, like me, he soon felt like a conventional middle-class Chinese Australian living in Sydney. He too was shocked by the amount of wealth that had poured in from China since the late 2000s. Fortunately, he had started working and purchasing properties way before I had, so he probably wasn't as pressured as I was by the soaring property prices driven by the overseas investors.

What made C's story more amazing than mine was his religious belief. I was quite surprised to discover that he was a Christian, and that he had been a Christian since the early 1990s when he was still in China. C described to me a very different China from before I was born, a version of China I had never known. In the late 1980s when he was a child, C told me, China was actually a very open country. Popular western culture flooded China from the US, Japan and Hong Kong. Political debate was much freer than it is today. People liked rock music and parties. People gathered together to criticise the government and the leaders, just as people did in any western country.

All sorts of social, political and religious ideas recovered from the impact of the Cultural Revolution and started to grow again. Then, when he was in high school in 1989, after the Tiananmen Square event, things seized up again—at least publicly. At university he was invited by a friend to join a secret Christian church, and he soon converted. His church remains underground in China even today.

C is certain there are a large number of Gen X Chinese who, like him, still have an open mind shaped during those years. I think he grew up more freely than I ever did.

C described to me his generation's views of Australia and the western world. His generation had seen the western world through TV and magazines since 1980. They believed that the west, including Japan, was much more advanced than China and that China should learn from the west and follow their lead. This kind of 'xenophilia' was a very common mindset in the 1980s. It makes me wonder how much the belief in Christianity was responsible for his generation's admiration of western culture.

Still, it was good to discover that his generation had something they believed in. This was much harder for my generation, because after 1989 western culture became more heavily regulated, and there seemed to be no legitimate, untarnished substitutes inside China. I could see that C was proud of his generation for their free-thinking mindset when compared with the generations before and after them.

CHINESE BABY BOOMERS

Last but not least, let's turn to the Chinese baby boomers. The reason I have placed them last is that this generation of new Chinese were not commonly seen overseas until very recently. When they were young, getting an education, let alone studying or travelling overseas, was almost impossible. Many of those who did make it out of China to countries such as Australia actually defected at great risk. Their stories are well known. Instead of covering this well-trodden ground, let's look at some statistics that can help put those stories in context.

The historical events that defined that generation spanned from the establishment of the People's Republic of China (the new China) in 1949 to the beginning of the Cultural Revolution in 1966. During this period the Chinese population grew by 19.2 per cent, from 583 million (1953 census) to 694 million (1964 census). Due to the inertia of the high birth rate and the rapidly improving medical conditions from 1965 to 1979 (the beginning of birth control, or the 'one-child policy'), the hyper population growth rose to the next level. In this period, the Chinese population grew from 694 million to 1008 million (1982 census), or over 45 per cent. Therefore, when talking about the high birth rate and population growth, the 'boomer generation' might more usefully be defined as those who were born between 1949 and 1979, just before the one-child policy was instituted.

The end of the civil war brought peace to mainland China, but the economy struggled and was unable to match those in the western world in the same period. As in the Soviet Union, a strong focus on industry—and especially on defence and heavy industry—and a dysfunctional social system resulted in low agricultural productivity. Between 1959 and 1961 the three-year-long Great Famine ravaged the country. The government estimated the number of unnatural deaths caused by food shortages during this period was about 15 million. Independent researchers have suggested much higher numbers, up to almost double the official figure.

Whatever the truth, the numbers were huge, and the psychological impact on people's minds was even greater. When my parents were between the ages of two and five, there simply was not enough food to feed the whole country, and people were starving to death every day. It probably had an even greater impact on people older than my parents. Even after the famine, China, still a poor country, was barely able to produce enough food for everyone. Everything was centrally planned and controlled. The lack of resources shaped the value system of my parents' generation. To grow food, to work harder and to make more money: these values were all-encompassing because the people understood too well how fragile life was, and how when those material resources ran out, life would just stop.

Despite three years of national famine, the population grew by almost 20 per cent before the start of the Cultural Revolution. In my opinion, what drove this growth was a combination of Chinese tradition and deliberate political policy. Traditionally, the Chinese favoured big families. The more workers a family had, the more food it could produce.

Many children meant a prosperous family, something to be proud of. People also got married very young in those days. For instance, my grandparents married when they were just 13 years old; they had my oldest uncle when they were 15. This might sound unbelievable today in Australia or in China, but it was absolutely normal in the old days in a Chinese village.

In a time when higher education was beyond reach, getting the kids married during their teenage years was probably not a bad idea. It meant most Chinese women could start having children eight years earlier than they do today. Research published in 2010 showed that the average age for Chinese women to have their first child was 23. It is probably over 25 now, and as high as 28 to 30 in some city areas.

In addition to the Chinese tradition of early marriage in rural areas, where most Chinese lived in the 1950s and 1960s, Chairman Mao believed that the key reason we had been able to thwart the Japanese invasion during World War II was sheer numbers. In 1950 Japan's population stood at just over 80 million—less than one-fifth of China's. Mao strongly encouraged Chinese families to have more babies, over the objections of some famous Chinese economists and scholars.

This direction was greatly influenced by similar policies in the Soviet Union, where having more children was also strongly encouraged. Women with lots of kids were crowned as 'Hero Mothers' in both the USSR and China. Our national birth rate was as high as 5.7 to 5.9 during this period. My father had six brothers and sisters. My mother's side did less well, but still she had four brothers and sisters. That was a standard for the whole country. This high birth rate continued into the 1960s and 1970s.

There are simply too many stories to tell of their generation. Those great changes I experienced when I grew up—it was my parents' generation and Gen X that made them happen. Because there is so much to talk about, I have chosen not to talk about it at all. Also, it is not what my friends in Australia are interested in. What they want to know is if these Chinese are relevant to Australia. And the answer is yes indeed, those Chinese are very relevant.

Although most baby boomers and Gen Xers had few opportunities to travel to other countries, they were willing to pay vast sums to send their children to study overseas. That has made an important contribution to the Australian higher education industry over the past decade. Not only did they sponsor their children to study overseas, but they also generously helped their children with the deposits they needed to purchase properties overseas where they chose to settle.

Maintaining another Chinese tradition, in addition to financial assistance, they believed they were responsible for raising their grandchildren. In several residential areas in Sydney with a high Chinese population density, you can see many Chinese grandparents with young kids in the playgrounds and the church playgroups. And they did not come here only to raise their grandchildren; they came to retire and, in turn, to be taken care of by their children. That might explain why property prices in cities with high Chinese migrant populations such as Sydney reach crazier levels than other cities in Australia, especially in suburbs with excellent schools, which are preferred by Chinese families regardless of the cost.

CHAPTER SUMMARY

- Chinese baby boomers were born and grew up in the turbulent early years of the People's Republic, which were marked by harsh living conditions, food shortages and famine—conditions that deeply affected this generation's patterns of behaviour.

- Chinese Gen Xers were born during the Cultural Revolution but grew up in the hopeful years that followed, a more open time when social, political and even religious ideas were reawakened.

- Born in the 1980s, the 80-hou generation grew up in a rapidly changing environment.

- The scale and speed of change meant the material living conditions of the 90-hou generation were vastly improved. The middle class were better off and had more opportunities, but generally had no interest in politics.

CHAPTER 4

CHINESE-STYLE DEMOCRACY

THE DILEMMAS

About 10 years ago, while I was still a young student, I sat next to a nice Australian lady on my flight from Beijing to Sydney. She was curious about overseas students from China like me. It was a 13-hour flight and there was not much else to do, so we talked a lot about Australia and China. She had visited many tourist locations in China during her trip. She told me she had even touched a panda in Sichuan.

This surprised me because normally no one is allowed to touch a panda. They are an endangered species: there are fewer than 2000 pandas alive today. They look so cute that everyone wants to get close to them, but if tourists were permitted to touch them, this contact alone could kill them all. It is not easy to get too close to them. There are normally one or two of them in each zoo in a fenced exhibition area far away from the tourists. Yes, Sichuan is the home territory of pandas and there could be many of them there, but I have never in my life heard of a tourist being allowed to touch one. So I asked her how she had managed it. She said their tour guide was a well-connected guy. He had bribed the director of the panda care centre so his tour group could touch the pandas. Of course, the bribe was paid by the tourists as part of the tour booking fee.

The panda story shocked me, but bribery in China in 2004 did not. It was just a part of daily life, almost boring. We talked more about China, and she raised another topic that astonished me. Indeed, in all my 22 years of life I had never heard anything like it. She asked me why China had invaded Tibet. Was it purely to create a military buffer zone? What was the human rights situation in Tibet today? On and on.

I remember sitting there staring at her and wondering if my poor command of English could explain why I did not understand her questions. I had a million question marks circling around in my head. I wondered where this stuff on Tibet came from. Her initial question alone, not to mention her version of Tibetan history, left me feeling disoriented. If any of it was true, why had I not known about such issues and what else did I not know? So the first thing I did when I got home was to get onto Google to learn some Chinese history that was never taught in China.

As I have puzzled over how to write about the politics and recent history of China, I have found myself facing a few serious dilemmas. Should I review the full political history since 1949 and risk getting my book banned in my own home country, or should I leave a few blanks there? Should I voice my true feelings and take the risk of offending some people, or should I maintain a careful political neutrality and leave those people undisturbed? This decision is a difficult one. I don't think there are any correct answers to questions such as this. There are just consequences, often unforeseeable, that must be faced once the decision has been made.

In 1977 the Chinese leadership faced a dilemma called the 'Two Whatevers'. CPC Chairman Hua Guofeng, Mao's successor, made the following statement: 'We will resolutely uphold whatever policy decisions Chairman Mao made and unswervingly follow whatever instructions Chairman Mao gave.' This statement almost dissuaded Deng Xiaoping from returning to the political arena. Without Deng's reforms China might have remained a poor communist country like North Korea even today. The communist leadership had to decide between endorsing Deng's policy and supporting Hua's rigid, 'politically correct' 'Two Whatevers'. Thankfully they supported Deng, and over the next 10 years China witnessed growth on an almost magical scale, as described in chapter 2.

I think I need to spend a little time on the politics of China because most Australians do not really understand it. In 2014, while I was working for a major accounting firm in Sydney, I attended a meeting in which a former Australian ambassador to China gave a presentation on the Chinese economy and politics. In the question-and-answer session, one of the firm's senior managers asked a question I found very amusing. Given the growing significance of major cities such as Beijing and Shanghai, he asked, was there a risk that those cities might declare independence and separate from China?

The fact he even raised that question told me how little he knew about China. While the UK could leave the European Union and Scotland can have a referendum to decide whether it remains in the UK, secession is simply not possible under the Chinese political system. The Chinese central government has a strong control over every province and every city in China. This system of central control was entrenched long before the new China came into being. Since the Qin dynasty, generations of emperors had refined the system to ensure the vast country did not fall apart (although it has from time to time, mostly in conjunction with foreign invasions).

Emperor Qin Shi Huang conquered the seven kingdoms of China and established the first Chinese empire in the third century BC. Perhaps his most important achievement was to standardise the diverse writing and measuring systems through-out the empire. This meant that, despite the hundreds of different languages and dialects in China, all imperial orders could be transmitted to the furthest reaches of the empire using the same written language.

The Han empire (206 BC – AD 220) reformed the feudal system and established counties to limit the power of the local lords. The lords fought back again and again, but the common goal of a single great unified empire always prevailed. The most significant improvement to the system occurred in the Song dynasty (969–1279), when the power to control armies was transferred from military to civil officials, and armies, regardless of where they were based, were loyal only to the emperor. Under the Ming dynasty (1368–1644), it was enshrined in law that military leaders were subordinate to civil leaders. The system was inherited by the Qing dynasty (1644–1911), who maintained it even through the twilight years of the empire and all the way to the Republic.

So throughout its long history it was unthinkable for a city to declare its independence from the empire. And this is even more true today given the strict rotation policies for army leaders. The purpose of rotation is to ensure that 'the generals do not know the soldiers, and the soldiers do not know the generals'. Every member of the People's Liberation Army, regardless of rank, follows orders only from their own commander—all the way up to the Central Military Commission.

This is why the real leader of China is not the president, but the Chairman of the Central Military Commission, who is also the General Secretary of the CPC, although usually the same person holds all three positions. One instance when this was not the case was during the transition from Deng Xiaoping to Jiang Zemin. After learning the lesson of 1989, and in the hope of a smooth political transition, the Politburo put Jiang in charge of the country, although Deng remained Chairman of the Central Military Commission for a few more years.

Having a strong, centrally controlled army is a double-edged sword. On the one hand, it helps to safeguard the country from foreign invasion and internal instability. On the other hand, influencing the people in power is a very difficult and risky project. In 1989 the Communist Party leadership faced another dilemma. I am not going to rehash old news that you probably already know or can easily glean from Wikipedia. I am only going to talk about the consequences of their decision.

After the political instability ended, China enjoyed another 10 years of hyper economic growth, as seen by the world. Across the country many people have benefited from the growing economy, including many who had participated directly in the 1989 event but remained in China afterwards. A significant number of others left China at that time and sought political asylum in western countries such as Australia. Ten years later, in 1999, another momentous political event occurred in China that drove many people to leave China and seek political asylum in the United States or Australia. Unlike 1989, this time it was not a dilemma for the communist leadership. It was probably a simple decision. I believe they had learned from the earlier event that uninterrupted growth of the Chinese economy depended on absolute political control. When a social group gets so big as to potentially threaten the control of the central government, there would be no hesitation in acting to neutralise it.

I had witnessed the event as a teenager in Beijing. There was controversy of course, and a great deal of resistance too. This opposition group was well funded; even today they remain active in every major Chinatown around the world. They publish newspapers and hold many gatherings. They may never have a chance to change what is happening inside China, but they have certainly focused the attention of the western world on 'human rights' issues in China.

HUMAN RIGHTS IN CHINA

China is often criticised by the western world, including Australia, for its poor record on human rights. Tibet, censorship, birth control, elections … it is a long list. I have no comments to make on these issues, but I would like to share an interesting insight from the point of view of the new generation of Chinese. I too feel there are human rights issues in China, but the list I have is quite different from those raised by a typical westerner.

During the Great Chinese Famine of 1958–1961 (and many years after that), the only human right that was relevant to every Chinese was the right to food, without which there could be no life or any other human rights. For my father's generation, therefore, the question of human rights was simple. As soon as the craziness stopped and people could focus on growing food and pushing back hunger, they were happy with their human rights.

With over 2000 years of history of being governed by an absolute ruler, ordinary Chinese cannot care less about who is their supreme leader.

Throughout Chinese history, politics has been the business of politicians (the nobles and royals) and not of ordinary Chinese people. They wanted no part in politics. All they ever wanted was to live peacefully and sufficiently. The people are happy with any leader who can offer them this. It does not matter to them that the leader prosecuted all the opposition, or that he killed his own brothers, or that she strangled her own daughter to gain political advantage (all real historical examples). It also does not matter if the leader has mistreated people in the past. The Chinese people are very good at forgiving and forgetting. They challenge the government only in rare and extreme cases (for example, when facing the option to fight or to die).

This might sound shocking to a modern westerner or even a modern Chinese, but it goes to the core of Confucianism — obedience. 'As children, we must obey our fathers. As wives, we must obey our husbands. As people, we must obey our Ruler.' As oppressive as this might sound to you, this is the fundamental Confucian philosophy, a set of ideas that has dominated the minds of the Chinese people for almost 20 centuries. (It is easy to see why China's rulers have supported a philosophy whose core principles are duty and obedience at all levels.)

To many conservative people a hundred years ago, democracy was a mad idea. It would have undermined their duty simply to obey, which they conceived of almost as a 'human right'. The mere thought of a popular election made them uncomfortable. The fact that the idea had been brought to China by foreigners made them even more uncomfortable. When Sun Zhongshan ended the Qing monarchy and founded the Republic of China, most Chinese would have thought of him as just another emperor, and they could live with that. A great many people conceived of Chairman Mao as emperor of the new China. During the Cultural Revolution he was worshipped as a god. If you challenged them to stop, they would fight you for taking away their 'human right to worship'.

Democracy still sounds crazy to the old generation, but it sounds pretty cool to the young people, just as communism sounded cool to the young people in the 1920s. Sun Zhongshan did not lead the Republic for long, and his successors were corrupt and autocratic. China faced many problems, including foreign invasion. The Communist Party vanguard proposed radical reforms that quickly gained them popularity.

The concept of equal distribution of wealth was naive but appealing to young minds, especially to those who had nothing. I can imagine what it would have felt like when young students talked about communism in the 1920s: just like when Sun shared his visions of a republic, and like how young Chinese student leaders talked about western democracy in 1989. To these young people, it was a dream, a goal worth pursuing, an ideal worth fighting and dying for. The republic, communism, western democracy, fundamentally different though they are, all have one thing in common: all are foreign ideas that were brought into China and threatened to subvert the traditional Chinese values. Can I call this a foreign invasion of the Chinese mind?

The interesting thing is that once people are infected with new ideas, it is pretty hard to turn them back. After the Cultural Revolution the leadership of the CPC resolved never again to give absolute power to the leader. The 'Chairman' of the CPC is now the 'General Secretary'. Decisions are no longer made by one person (whether an emperor or a chairman), but by a leadership team.

The conflict within that leadership team had fuelled the debate when the idea of western democracy entered China again after the Cultural Revolution. The 1989 event might not have played out as the students had hoped, but it reminded the leadership powerfully of the importance of ideology. Ever since the death of Chairman Mao, China has experienced a critical vacuum of beliefs. All the traditional values and religious ideas had been greatly damaged during the Cultural Revolution, and remain highly regulated to this day.

So what is the one value system that the Chinese government is likely to propose today in order to unite the country? Is it still communism or socialism? The official statistics tell us there are 87 million Communist Party members in China. In reality, many who claim to be communists do not really understand, believe or act according to communist principles. The remaining 1.4 billion–plus people do not call themselves communists. To be honest, I think the only cultural bond for the entire country is the economy—in other words, money. Call it realism, if you want to make it sound philosophical. Realistically, democracy is not as relevant as the distribution of social wealth.

As long as people can make money, which party runs the country is of little concern to the ordinary people. It is interesting to see that the Chinese government has started to promote Confucian ideas again and has established a great many Confucian academies around the world. Confucianism was heavily attacked by the CPC during the Cultural Revolution, because, like Christianity and Buddhism, it is incompatible with communism or socialism, under which banner the current Chinese government still operates. This makes me, and anyone who understands the essence of Confucianism, wonder about the motives of this new promotion.

FROM ENTHUSIASM TO REALISM

My wife, Zhen, told me this story about my father-in-law. She heard it from her aunt, because her father never talked about anything that happened during the Cultural Revolution. When he was a student leader in 1968, he was captured by his political opponents. (In the civil riot, both sides claimed to be loyal supporters of Chairman Mao and accused the other of being traitors and counter-revolutionists.) He was bound and escorted onto a stage on the campus and 'put on trial' by the mob. He screamed out on the stage: 'I am not a traitor! I am not a counter-revolutionist!'

But no one cared. So he was thrown into jail. Later he was exiled to the villages, together with many young people from the city. He was very lucky not to have been killed. Instead he was sentenced to spend 10 years in the village before being allowed to return to the city at the end of the Cultural Revolution. He had learned his lesson about the risk of political enthusiasm. He never talked about his experience or about politics for the rest of his life.

When Zhen was in the seventh grade, she was unhappy with the school's arrangement for extended study hours. She stood up and asked her fellow classmates to join her in a student strike to force the headmaster to listen to them. Her teacher reported her to her father, and her father smacked her hard (it is quite normal for Chinese parents to smack their kids, even today) and warned her never to do it again, or to get involved with anything that sounded like a political demonstration. I can understand that his action was aimed at protecting his daughter, given that she was young and passionate about her rights. He understood the risk of being politically active in China more than most people did; he would not see his beloved daughter going down the same path.

Forty years have passed since the end of the Cultural Revolution, but politics remains a sensitive topic in China. As I have already noted, I am conscious of the need to be very careful when I write about the political history, having no desire to produce a controversial book that could get banned in my own country. I would avoid political topics altogether if it was possible. Unfortunately, when you talk about China, no matter what the topic, it is always related to politics.

I cannot help wondering why this is the case. One of my theories is that there are simply too many people in China. When you have people, you have politics. And when you have so many people, you cannot get anything done without politics. Many Chinese people do not realise this. The Gen Y Chinese I interviewed for this book, especially the younger ones, are quite indifferent to politics. They have never cast a vote in their entire life. They have no interest in watching *CCTV News*. They would prefer to spend time playing Pokémon Go rather than talking about Chinese politics.

This is so different from my parents' generation, where everyone was involved in the Cultural Revolution (willingly or unwillingly) and lived under strong political control. It is also different from my cousin's generation (the Gen X Chinese), who had demonstrated such a strong passion and sense of social responsibility in 1989, risking their lives and futures by marching in the streets and demanding western-style democratic reforms. They might not have done it in the right way, but at least they played an important part in the country's political conversation.

What has happened to my generation that has made most of us so indifferent to politics? The answer is found in the new religion of China—realism. After their early political engagement, the boomers and Gen X Chinese (those who remained in China) all became realists. They recognised that their passion for politics would achieve little and was very dangerous for them, so they stepped back. And they never wanted their children to follow the same perilous path. They focused instead on creating personal wealth so they could send their children overseas—to developed countries that take western democracy and political stability for granted.

As a result of this transition, recent Chinese political history is not taught in detail at school or talked about in Chinese homes. Ask a political question of a Chinese kid who has just graduated from college and flown to Australia for further studies and the only response you are likely to get is a look of confusion, which is all I could offer when questioned on Tibet on that flight all those years ago.

That question opened a door for me. I was curious, and I love history. So I went online and searched for information I could never have accessed in China. After I had read everything I could find I was furious, and confused. It was incredible to me that those things actually happened, and that they were concealed so well from my generation (and the generations after me). I could not believe the Chinese were so 'realistic' today and yet had zero interest in knowing about their own political inheritance.

It was kind of lucky that the pressures of job seeking and getting married and having kids greatly distracted me from my passion for politics. I had quickly been transformed from a young and passionate student to a father and husband with an absolute responsibility for his family. Only then did I fully realise why most Chinese these days do not demonstrate the political passion they had once had.

The truth is, when we become adults, we have too much to lose. In the past 30 years, most Chinese people have acquired their own properties. They have plenty of money, which would quickly depreciate in the event of any political instability.

They have stable jobs, and they need those jobs to repay their mortgage. They are stuck in the details of life, and the impulse to 'make the world a better place' has been buried deep beneath the pressing realities of the present.

That is the moment when an enthusiast becomes a realist. Only those who have nothing to lose can afford another revolution. The greater the number of middle-class people we have in China, the more stable China will become. The Chinese government deserves a big round of applause for creating so many middle-class families in China in the past few decades.

Any radicals seeking to overturn the current system will meet with ever greater resistance from middle-class Chinese, whose 'human right' to continue being middle class is challenged by such idealism. Together with the glorious restoration of traditional Confucian beliefs, the new leadership seems to have found just the right formula to manage this huge country.

THE REALITY

When I look at China, the only reality I see is non stop change. When I returned for a short while in 2010, corruption was still the norm. There were thousands of high-end restaurants and private clubs across the country whose main clientele were government officials. For anyone who worked in the government system, not taking bribes was seen as hypocritical. People like that could be excluded from the circle and see their careers stalled.

Although corruption was illegal and carried heavy penalties, including the death sentence, it was so universal that no one really thought about the consequences. We used to joke in China that if we lined up all the civil servants and shot them, we risked killing a few truly innocent ones, but if we shot every second one, many of the bad ones would get away. Bribery was a legitimate cost associated with doing any business in China. Even multinational companies knew they had to bend the rules to fit in with the Chinese reality in order to win certain contracts and develop their business in China.

As someone who had finished his education and worked in Australia, I felt highly disappointed with the corrupt system. I had no hesitation in distancing myself from that reality. What neither I nor most Chinese saw coming was the rapid change that took place in 2013, when President Xi Jinping assumed office. In a sweeping anti-corruption campaign, more than 170 high-ranked government and military officials (including five national leaders) were arrested, and over 100000 public servants nationwide were indicted for corruption. The move sent shockwaves through the country and made it clear that corruption was no longer acceptable in China.

The official Chinese news network declared that President Xi had gained overwhelming support from the Chinese people. I don't know where that information came from, because Chinese people still do not vote or poll, but I completely believe in the truth of it. The civil servants are a minority, and the people (especially those who have to pay out in bribes) are in the majority. For ordinary Chinese citizens, a corruption-free country is naturally a much better place in which to live.

This is also a big change for foreigners wishing to do business with the Chinese, especially state-owned companies. Up to 2012 I would probably have suggested they respect and accept the realities and budget for 'relationship building' if they wished to do business in China. Today I would advise against payment of any money to Chinese government or corporate officials, because anything that looks like bribery will be turned down immediately. Having said that, relationship building is still an important part of doing business with or in China. It just has evolved to a more sophisticated and civilised level.

Another reality that foreigners need to be aware of is the growing sense of patriotism and nationalism of the Chinese people, including those living in Australia. The first instance of this I can remember occurred in 1999, when NATO forces led by the US bombed the Chinese embassy in Belgrade, killing three Chinese journalists. The Chinese public were outraged. Organised demonstrations (the people probably came voluntarily, but the event itself was organised by the government) encircled US embassies and consulates in major cities.

These were the first large-scale public gatherings and demonstrations since 1989. There were many domestic concerns over which people would have loved to take to the streets, but it was too risky. Here was a perfect opportunity to let off steam, and a safe vent for the government too. The demonstrations were contained by massive security to make sure things did not go out of control. But while the protests were carefully managed, the anger towards the US for bombing our embassy was very real. The Chinese, especially those who had fought in the Korean War, really hated the United States for being an 'international bully' and forcibly interfering in other countries' affairs. This went beyond their love for American democracy and popular culture.

A similar flashpoint occurred in 2012 during a territorial dispute with Japan over the uninhabited Diaoyu dao Islands. This time there was some serious damage to Japanese businesses in China. Many Japanese-brand cars (even though they had been made in China and were owned by Chinese) were damaged during the riot. No Japanese citizens were hurt, but some Chinese driving Japanese cars were seriously injured. I believe the Chinese public are not always very rational and mature in political demonstrations, but can you blame them? They were never given the opportunity to demonstrate in China. Only protests against foreign countries were allowed. I hope they do not have recourse to practise more of those.

Patriotism, in China as overseas, grows out of some combination of government propaganda and the true feelings of the people. As the new generation of Chinese, we have witnessed the huge change in China over the past 30 years, change that has been largely unseen or misunderstood by the western world.

One example of this is the 2008 Beijing Olympics. When the torch passed through Canberra, protests were organised against China's hosting the Olympic Games.

The main target was human rights problems in China. The protesters felt that the western world should have boycotted the Beijing Olympics. Most of the protesters were Chinese living in Australia who did not agree with the then Chinese government. This is pretty normal. You can find these protesters outside the Chinese embassy too. What was not normal was that many of my friends from China gathered in Canberra to 'guard the torch' and protest against those anti-China demonstrators. And they were doing so voluntarily, because hosting an Olympics for the first time meant a lot to the Chinese people.

This, in my opinion, indicates an extremely positive patriotic attitude that should be encouraged. The Chinese living in Australia have more freedom to express their opinions in civilised ways, including through peaceful gatherings and demonstrations. This is something that should be permitted inside China, too.

Returning to reality, China is less corrupt than it used to be (I don't think corruption is completely wiped out; even the state media would say fighting corruption is a long battle), which is good news for Australian businesses. The new generation of Chinese are prouder of their native country than those who arrived in Australia 20 to 30 years ago; this has nothing to do with their feelings about the government.

They do not like to hear anyone, including the mainstream Australian media, describe China as an extreme communist country, because it simply is not true. They probably will not be offended if you describe the Chinese as realists, because they mostly are. They will be offended if you tell them that the South China Sea does not belong to China, even though they personally do not own a single drop of water in that sea.

CHAPTER SUMMARY

- Strong, centralised political control, and subordination of military to civil leaders—these core unifying principles were entrenched long before the new China came into being.

- Uninterrupted economic growth in the 1980s and 1990s depended on absolute political control. Two acts of political defiance, in 1989 and 1999, confirmed this view for China's leaders.

- For those brought up on Confucian principles of duty and obedience and 2000 years of absolute rule, democracy was inconceivable.

- Today the dominant value system is not communism but realism. Politics is generally a source of indifference and democracy is less relevant than wealth distribution.

- Growing economic security for middle-class Chinese and reduction of corruption since 2013 have helped create new levels of national pride and patriotism.

CHAPTER 5

WHAT DO THE NEW CHINESE BELIEVE?

FOLK BELIEFS AND SUPERSTITION

When I was a student, I lived in a small rental unit near Macquarie University. It was old, built in the 1960s, without any access control, so anyone could walk up for some door-to-door selling. One early morning I was sleeping in when someone buzzed my door. I got up quickly and opened the door without much thought. In a safe country such as Australia, I reckoned, it really wasn't necessary to check a visitor's identity before opening up. So I found this lovely young couple standing there. They asked me a lot of questions I didn't understand, perhaps through a combination of my poor English and their particular religious vocabulary. They were very patient, though. At the time I was not sure which church they belonged to, but now I think they were probably Jehovah's Witnesses.

They were truly nice, like people I could not turn down for any reason. But I'm not religious—I am simply not interested. While they were talking, I was thinking of the right words to politely reject them without leaving any opportunity for further questions. This was important, because at the time I was myself doing door-to-door sales for a mobile phone company, so I knew how salespeople prepared their pitch. If I said I was not religious and had no spiritual belief of any kind, they would have plenty of follow-up questions to get me to buy in. I had to shut them down quickly so I could go back to my bed.

So I said, 'Thank you so much for telling me all these wonderful things, but I am a Buddhist.' It was a good response. It stopped them in their tracks. They probably had no idea about Buddhism and were not sure if things could get ugly if they pressed me any further. So they politely said goodbye and moved on to another door. Closing the door, I thought I had been very smart. I had no compunction about lying. For another 10 years, I never thought about my beliefs again.

If you want to define the national religion for China, it should be called Superstitionism. The Chinese are very superstitious, and I'm not just talking about the older generation. First, let's have a look at the traditional religions in China. The dominant religion in China is not Taoism or Buddhism; it is Chinese folk religion.

Folk religion is not a systematic religion, but rather a collection of various supernatural beliefs scattered across the country. You can worship the Jade Deity (the highest god, who governs the heavens as the emperor governs the earth), or you can pray to your ancestor for blessings. You can worship Mazu, who protects the seas and sailors, or the Dragon King, who controls the rain. You can worship a star in the sky called Wenquxing, which will help you get good results in an exam; or you can pray directly to the mud to ask for a good harvest. In this polytheistic system, it is believed that there is a supernatural spirit in everything (the mountains, the rivers, a snake, a turtle, even a flower). Some spirits can be very powerful; you might not want to pray to them, but you certainly do not want to offend them.

Although most people do not think about it and just go to various temples to pray for things, there is actually a kind of structure or system governing folk religion. This structure was first recorded only in the Ming dynasty in two novels. One,

Investiture of the Gods, was written around 1550. The narrative began at the end of the Shang dynasty (about 1027 BC), when the King of Zhou fought the tyrant and established the Zhou dynasty in China. Many of the dead generals, including the Prince of Zhou, were made gods after the investiture of the prime minister of the Zhou King, Jiang Ziya, who was endowed by heaven with supernatural powers.

Because of his sacrifices and leadership, the Prince of Zhou became the Jade Deity, who ruled heaven. All the other generals were given important roles in the Heavenly Court, which governed the universe. You can see them at night as stars.

In another famous novel, *Journey to the West*, published around 1592, Buddhism was integrated into Chinese folk religion. Based on a true story, the book tells of the famous monk Xuanzang (AD 602–664) in the Tang dynasty who travelled a long way from China to India to learn true Buddhism and bring back to China the original Buddhist Sutras. In this book, the Buddha was described as a super-powerful god who lived in the west and ran the universe through his ultimate power source, the Dharma.

There was a rebellious character known as the Monkey King, who fought the army of the Heavenly Court. The Jade Deity was in big trouble because he could not control this Monkey. As a last resort, he requested help from the Buddha, who overpowers the Monkey King with the palm of his hand. To redeem his sin, the Monkey King was condemned to escort Xuanzang to India. They experienced numerous adversities on the journey but finally secured the Sutras and brought them back to China.

This novel has had great significance for Chinese religion and culture. It established the belief for generations of Chinese that the Buddha is the highest and most powerful supernatural being, stronger than any of the native Chinese gods. It is interesting that even though Buddhism originated in India, it has been embraced by the Chinese for so long that no one thinks of it as a foreign implant. Although most Chinese today are not Buddhists, their respect for the Buddha has persisted. This is true for the new Chinese, the Chinese in other parts of the world, and even those who call themselves communists or atheists.

Because of the strong influence of folk religion, Buddhism in China has become more superstitious compared with the Buddha's original teachings. When I told the JW couple I was a Buddhist, I lied. But many years later, when I researched Buddhism, I was shocked to learn that the Buddha was not a god but a human being whose only superpower was exerted through the ultimate wisdom of the *dharma*. I came to realise that the Chinese tradition of worshipping the Buddha and praying to him or to the bodhisattvas (Buddha's assistants) for the birth of a boy or for more money or for longevity was totally wrong. The Chinese form of worship is based on superstition rather than Buddhist philosophy.

The other traditional Chinese religion, Taoism, whose origins were again quite philosophical and natural, has also been heavily contaminated by superstitious practices from folk beliefs. The ultimate goal of Taoist practice is to achieve immortality—in other words, to become a god. This idea was very appealing to some kings and emperors.

The first emperor of China, Qin Shi Huang, employed many Taoist priests to comb through the ancient texts and search the world for the elixir of life that would give him immortality. Among the many outlandish solutions the priests proposed was having sex with hundreds of young virgins, which might indeed have contributed to the emperor's early death. They experimented with 'immortality pills' by mixing different chemicals. During one of these experiments, the mix exploded powerfully. That is the story of how the Chinese invented gunpowder. Over the following 2000 years, some Taoist practitioners continued to believe in and work on the elusive elixir.

I have heard stories that suggest Chairman Mao was superstitious all his life. After the civil war he once visited a temple where the abbot was said to have prophetic powers. Mao asked the abbot to foretell his future. The abbot wrote a number on a piece of paper and gave it to Mao. On it was written (in Chinese characters) 8341, but the abbot would offer no further explanation. After the visit, Mao decided to change the code for the PLA Chinese Central Safeguard Regiment to 8341.

The 8341 Special Regiment continued to guard the Chairman until he died. And only then did everyone understand the meaning of these numbers. Mao had lived for 83 years and had been in power for 41 years (dated from the Zunyi Conference, which established his authority in the CPC, until his death). Of course the Chinese government would deny this story, but it is true that '8341' was completely at odds with all existing army coding schemes back then, so many people choose to believe it.

THE DOCTRINE OF THE MEAN

I talk about the principle of obedience in chapter 4; another core Confucian idea is called the Doctrine of the Mean. The principle of obedience describes the ideal relationship between people in a system — there must be a universally accepted chain of command for a society to function (the three obediences). The Doctrine of the Mean, on the other hand, tells everyone how they should appear and act, especially among their peers.

The Doctrine of the Mean was originally mentioned in a book by one of Confucius's grandchildren. The treatise itself was ambiguous; numerous scholars through history have annotated and attempted to explain it. Those interpretations shaped the idea into what it is today. I am by no means an authority on Confucianism, so please don't quote my interpretation of the Doctrine of the Mean. You can find many different versions online. What I am describing here is only how a normal educated person from China would interpret the doctrine and act in accordance with that understanding.

In essence, the Doctrine of the Mean might be boiled down to 'being modest and humble'. As good Chinese, we are expected to obey those we should obey, and to be modest and humble among our peers. We should focus on our own development and learning, but not brag about it. We should put ideas in writing and publish quietly, rather than announcing them in front of a big audience. We should sit quietly and listen to our teachers, rather than asking questions, which is an act of disrespect and vanity. We should not engage in debate, but always remain quiet and calm. If we play an important role in a team, we should be humble and let others take the credit. We should be satisfied with what we have, instead of greedily seeking more. If we participate in a competition, we should always be modest and well mannered.

This is my interpretation of the Doctrine of the Mean, and I am confident that most new Chinese (who have not done any scholarly research on the Confucian theory) would agree with me.

From this you can probably guess why most educated adults a hundred years ago would have hated the idea of democracy, which involves a lot of public speaking, debates and strenuous, even aggressive advocacy. This is totally against Confucius's teaching of what constitutes being a good man. And the fact that the younger students even involved women in public speaking and demands for rights—well, that was totally unacceptable.

Women in China had their own chain of obedience: 'As daughters we must obey our fathers; as wives we must obey our husbands; as widows we must obey our sons.' Both democracy and communism would encourage women to speak out publicly about their rights and demonstrate brazenly against the emperor or the government. This is total madness in a Confucian society. Imagine one day going out and seeing that everyone on the street and on the train was stark naked—that was the level of shock the new ideas would have caused among the old Chinese a hundred years ago.

But ultimately, backed by popular demand, democracy and communism did win in China. Both the Republic and the

Communist government completely scrapped the Confucian education and exam system, replacing it with a modern school system introduced from the west. Since then the Doctrine of the Mean has become a derogatory term. It is used by the younger generation of Chinese to criticise Confucian theory and mock the conservative old scholars.

People are encouraged to express their ideas. Women are encouraged to work outside the home and advocate for their rights. As a matter of fact, if you ask me for one good thing that the CPC did in China, my answer would be *it set women free from men*. And not only free, but in many cases women probably have had greater authority than men. For example, for most of Chinese history girls were banned from receiving education. Today girls not only go to school, but do better than boys in many ways. Women not only choose freely who they will marry, but also control the family in its two most important and decisive areas: finance and education. This is in great contrast to the situation in China a hundred years ago. Many people may not agree with my statement, but that's okay, because I am going to follow the Doctrine of the Mean here and not engage in debate.

The radical young Chinese may have despised the Doctrine of the Mean, but it is impossible to extinguish a 2000-year-old tradition overnight. In fact, the Doctrine of the Mean has never completely disappeared from Chinese education. It has been passed on through our blood and emerged in the new educational system. When I was a student in China, we had been prompted to follow the Doctrine of the Mean under the name of 'discipline'. We were taught the discipline of sitting in the classroom and listening quietly, of not raising our hand unless the teacher asked us to. We exert discipline when we withhold our views in public unless we are invited to speak.

This has had a big impact on politics in China. As I described in chapter 4, the baby boomers in China had tasted the bitter fruit of activism during the Cultural Revolution, and Gen Xers have bad memories of 1989. Both generations of adults probably figured out how important the Doctrine of the Mean still is in China. They would rather encourage their children to follow the doctrine in a modern way than to abandon it. Because that is what it takes to survive in China.

Many Australian lecturers who have taught international students from China will tell you that Chinese students are quiet and shy. That is absolutely true, especially for my generation. As I have discussed, that was the way we were taught when we grew up. In 2016 I returned to university, studying for a marketing degree at UNSW. What I discovered there was quite different from what I had experienced 10 years before.

The '90-hou' students from China speak much better English than most of my peers, and they are certainly a lot more active and engaged in the classroom. This could be due to the fact that these students are studying marketing (which might require a more outgoing personality than accounting). Or it could be because of a different university environment and entry requirements. But it could also be because the education system in China is changing, and the younger generation have been less influenced by the Doctrine of the Mean. They are still not as active and engaged as the local students, but I have definitely detected a change in that direction.

SCIENCE MEETS SUPERSTITION

I believe I am generally not superstitious, but I still need to play by the rules. For example, we once inspected a house for sale. It was a perfect house, ideal for our family and very stylish. The only problem was its street number, which was 74. In Chinese, 74 can mean 'angry to death' or 'die together' or 'wife dies'. I could not buy that house, and neither could most other Chinese.

Not surprisingly, that beautiful property failed at auction and was sold for a very low price, compared with similar properties sold to Chinese buyers at the time. The sellers could have avoided this disappointment if they had known something about Chinese numerology and unlucky numbers. This is just one example of how the decision making of less superstitious Chinese is affected by superstition. There are lots more examples. As we are born surrounded by the Chinese folk traditions, which essentially amount to a collection of superstitions, there is no way for us to totally live without them.

But most of the time we make rational decisions based on 'science'—at least we think we do. Besides realism, science is the only fundamental belief that most of the new Chinese could agree on, including those with a strong religious background. The reason I have brought science up in this chapter is to briefly discuss its influence on Chinese decision making regarding the destination for study overseas. When Sun Zhongshan established the Republic of China, he brought in two guests from the west: Mr Democracy and Mr Science. (These are the words used in our primary school history book.)

Mr Science represented the new ways of life (and war) that were totally foreign to the Chinese. At that time, lots of young Chinese left their homes to study in Europe and Japan. They chose Europe because it was seen as the centre of the world and the birthplace of science; and they chose Japan because of its proximity. The United States was probably the third choice, given it was a growing power that had not yet played an important role in world history. Countries such as Australia or Canada were not even on the list. The early generation of overseas students from China were seeking knowledge; most dreamed of using that knowledge to make China a better place.

Some of them succeeded, helping to transform China into something else—perhaps something better in their eyes. A hundred years later, my generation of Chinese who went to study in foreign countries were not thinking about another revolution in China. Studying overseas was normally bundled with the goal of migrating to these countries for a better life. Our choice of destination had less to do with science or other knowledge than with the potential for carving out a good life there.

A city that is very similar to Sydney in lifestyle is Vancouver, Canada. In the 1980s the most popular English textbook in China was *The Man from Vancouver*. A great many baby boomer and Gen X Chinese learned their English from that textbook. Few young people today know it because so many other English textbooks have appeared since the early 1990s. But their parents, those who funded these studies and migrations and property purchases, have fond memories of the city of Vancouver. For this reason, the city of Vancouver has experienced ridiculous property price hikes similar to those in Sydney. What influenced the Chinese who went there and purchased properties? In my opinion, besides all the advantages the city had to offer, the memory of an English textbook from their childhood.

Not long ago, I watched an SBS documentary about the rich Chinese in Vancouver. They showed an interview with a man who was the descendant of an early Cantonese Chinese settler in Canada. He runs a dragon dance school in Vancouver's Chinatown. He expressed his frustration that the new generation of Chinese has absolutely no interest in the traditional Chinese culture he keeps alive. Even worse, the new arrivals from China almost never even visit Chinatown.

It is surprising to me that Vancouver's Chinatown is run so badly that there is no reason for the new Chinese to visit. (The Chinatowns in Sydney and Melbourne are doing pretty well; I'll talk about why in a later chapter.) What is not surprising is that Canadians, SBS and that man of Cantonese Chinese ancestry have little understanding of the new Chinese. First of all, the dragon dance (or lion dance) is a tradition recognised in Guangdong province (where the Cantonese-speaking population lives) and only a few other places. Many provinces in China do not have that tradition.

And he was right, the communist government did erase some great Chinese culture, and the new generation of Chinese have very different interests and tastes from those Chinese who arrived in Vancouver over a hundred years ago. This is not too hard to understand. I don't think the French population in Quebec today would have many cultural bonds with the new generation of French living in France, either. The disconnect is obvious. What's wrong is the assumptions. The Canadians and that Cantonese man made the assumption that the dragon dance represents a traditional Chinese culture every Chinese would identify with; this is not correct.

The reason no new Chinese visit Chinatown in Vancouver is most likely because the restaurants there still serve old Cantonese food (which, by the way, tastes nothing like modern-day Cantonese food). It has nothing to do with tradition or culture. It is simply the science of marketing.

A new phenomenon today in China (and in some places overseas too) is to clothe superstition with science for marketing purposes. Most westerners are familiar with feng shui, a philosophical system closely connected to Taoism, and often used in fortune telling and property inspection today. A 'master' of feng shui claims to use the system intuitively to 'convert bad things to good things' in a way that appeals to Chinese consumers.

Many people (more Cantonese speakers than Mandarin speakers, from my observation) still have a strong belief in feng shui. And I can't deny that it often works. I like to think of it as part of the traditional culture and philosophical system. It annoys me, though, when someone attempts to create a 'science' out of such a traditional system in order to make money. Chinese do not like '4' in their phone number but believe '8' brings good fortune. Someone who was once my friend has sought to capitalise on this market with a new theory called 'the legend of numbers'. They are trying to use feng shui 'science' to explain why your mobile phone number could be bringing you bad luck, and how a different combination could bring you good fortune and health.

To me, that is loathsome. But even I can't deny that their dodgy strategy has been successful. They probably sell millions of dollars' worth of not-so-popular phone numbers, including ones with lots of 4s in them. I am sure they can market the property with a street number 74 very well by applying their new 'scientific' number theory.

DEALING WITH THE NEW CHINESE

It is actually pretty hard to avoid dealing with the new Chinese when you live in a city such as Sydney. You probably had a few friends at school who were of Chinese origin. And you probably found it was pretty easy to get along with them, because they were not very different from any other Australian. Dealing with the new Chinese from the new China can be a totally different experience.

You could be dealing with them in a personal or a professional context. You might want lots of new Chinese to come to your opal store to spend all they have, or you might want some giant Chinese company to acquire your farm at a premium price, or you might just need to tell your new Chinese neighbour to keep the noise down sometimes. Obviously, the things that would please or offend people are different from person to person. I will touch on only the basics here.

Speaking a person's native language is an easy way to reach anyone. Again I'll use Kevin Rudd as my example. I know most Chinese like him for no reason other than that he speaks fluent Mandarin. But you do not have to become a fluent speaker. A simple 'Nihao' (hello) and 'Xiexie' (thank you) could make a world of difference when you meet a Mandarin speaker from

China for the first time. They know you most likely know no Chinese, but your effort to greet them in Chinese is a gesture they will appreciate.

And spoken Chinese is not that hard to learn. Many primary schools and high schools in Sydney have introduced Mandarin classes already. I have worked with 100 per cent Caucasian Australians who have learned to speak fluent Mandarin after just a year of study in China. Yes, the four tones are a bit hard for English speakers, but the rest of the spoken language is much easier than English, with no changes in verb tense and almost no grammar. I would not recommend the written language, because it would probably take you a decade just to learn the basics!

Knowing where your guest is from is another connection point. Most people know Beijing and Shanghai already, but there are thousands of cities in China, some of which even I have never heard of. If my Chinese friend tells me the province it is in, though, I can place it roughly on the map. As an Australian you are not expected or required to know them all. If your guest is really important to you (for example, a potential Chinese investor willing to put millions into your company), you should make sure you find out.

This can be done with some simple research on Wikipedia. Just remember, there are 1.38 billion people in China, most of whom do not speak Cantonese. And really, you will only meet a small number of them in your lifetime—a small number of people, from a handful of cities. Think of *Game of Thrones*: if you can name the capitals of all the Seven Kingdoms without referring to Wikipedia, you are probably a loyal fan, but the people from Storm's End would not really expect you to know their hometown.

Recognising the changes in China and that China is no longer a poor and chaotic communist country is another really easy way to please your Chinese guest. What I find surprising is that most westerners still don't get it. Their image of the mainland Chinese is either of a poor peasant wearing an army-green Mao suit and clutching a copy of the Little Red Book, or of a poor student survivor of Tiananmen Square who has to wash dishes in Chinese restaurants for a living. Of course, once they have experienced a typical home auction in Sydney, they flip to the other extreme and see all Chinese as like the *fuerdai* (children of the super-rich), whose parents smuggled billions in cash out of China through illegal channels.

All these stereotypes either are dug up from the past or represent only a very rare breed. The vast majority of the new Chinese you see here are ordinary Chinese like me. We are skilled migrants who make an honest living here with only Australian-sourced income. We are not poor, but we are no richer than the average Australian. This applies to most Chinese tourists you meet in Australia, too. Travelling to Australia is no longer a luxury. And the tourists are not planning on overstaying their tourist visa to work illegally, because they have better things to do back in China.

So it is risky to make any assumptions about the Chinese you meet. Your best course is to do a little research. For example, if you are meeting a potential Chinese business partner, you can probably find some basic information on LinkedIn (a rare example of a western social media platform that is accessible in China) or by talking to other knowledgeable Chinese friends. As long as you don't make assumptions and you avoid stereotyping, your encounters with the new Chinese should go well.

One last point: Avoiding certain topics would probably please most of the new Chinese you meet. People have different views, not least on political matters. Unless you are participating in a debate in the UN, I see no reason why you need to persuade every new acquaintance of the typical Australian political view. As noted in chapter 3, most new Chinese of my generation and later probably don't have any idea of the recent history of China. All of them have subsisted on the same government propaganda their whole life, and their parents would not have discussed politics at home. Avoiding political topics will likely ensure your conversation with your new Chinese friend goes much, much more smoothly.

It is important to know that most of the new Chinese you are likely to meet here in Sydney are well educated and therefore should be reasonably easy to deal with. They might not all speak perfect English and they could sometimes be hard to understand, but all of them will certainly have made a great effort to learn, including those older Chinese who came here in their fifties or sixties. Not only have they learned the English language, but also they are trying very hard to fit into the local community and live according to Australian standards and common sense. So the easiest way to deal with the new Chinese is simply to be yourself—an authentic and open-minded Australian.

CHAPTER SUMMARY

- Traditionally, the dominant religion in China was not Taoism or Buddhism but folk religion, a diverse body of supernatural beliefs scattered across the country.

- Even the most pragmatic new Chinese are not immune to superstition.

- Confucian teachings on obedience, respect, modesty and humility were inconsistent with the idea of democracy, yet democracy and communism won through with popular support.

- After 60 years of communism, some of these deep-rooted ideas persist even among young Chinese, although as the education system has changed, their hold has lessened.

- Australian stereotypes of Chinese people and assumptions about those they may meet socially or professionally can be easily corrected with a little research and education.

CHAPTER 6

HOW DID CHINA GET SO RICH?

MADE IN CHINA

Anyone who has visited the country recently knows the growth in China is real, and very visible. In 1950 some 544 million people lived mostly in villages; by 2015, the population had ballooned to 1.38 billion people, with 56 per cent living in cities. The scale of the construction being carried out to accommodate this population growth is stunning. Besides housing, the new population needs food, clothing, transport, services and entertainment. The supply of every household product to its own population alone would make China the largest market by volume in the world.

Built on top of the traditional industries, China now has the world's largest telecommunication network. It has much faster internet than Australia, even in small towns in the country's relatively poor west. From one of the world's poorest undeveloped countries to the world's second largest economy, it is obvious that China has become rich mostly through real economic growth.

Even if you have never been to China, you can see the growth with your own eyes every day. An important part of this growth has been from exports to the rest of the world. While I wrote these words I looked around me in search of something in the room that was *not* made in China. I could not find much. I knew the microprocessor in my laptop was made in the United States. Some high-tech parts in my iPhone and Apple watch were made in the US, Japan or South Korea, but the final products were assembled in a factory in China and therefore also tagged 'Made in China'.

My clothes were made in China, as was my furniture, my TV and my fridge. The fresh food in my fridge was mostly locally grown, but I had some frozen food in the freezer that was produced in China and shipped to Australia mainly for Chinese consumers living here. This is probably the best evidence for an Australian of how the Chinese became so rich.

But do the Chinese get to keep all the profits from selling to the world? Definitely not. Although made in China, most of the products in my room were brands owned by global companies such as Apple, Sony, Samsung, Microsoft, IKEA and numerous other non-Chinese brands. They were made or assembled in China, transported to the port and shipped out of the country. The factory in China that made them gets a small cut of the profit. The transportation system gets a small cut too. The remaining profit goes to the brand owner and the distributors outside China.

Let's use the iPhone as an example. In their 2011 study 'Capturing Value in Global Networks', Kenneth Kraemer and other researchers found that for each iPhone sold, Apple took 58.5 per cent of the profit, non-Apple US companies took 2.4 per cent, South Korean companies took 4.7 per cent, while other parts were sourced from Japan, Taiwan and other countries. After the cost of input materials (21.9 per cent) and non-China labour (3.5 per cent), the Chinese factory ended up with proceeds from labour of just 1.8 per cent. Therefore, as the 'world's factory', China took only a tiny percentage of the profit, because they did not own the technology and brand. They were just poor labourers, not so different from the Chinese labourers who helped build the Pacific Railroad in the US.

Some Chinese are smart. Like the people from Wenzhou I mention in chapter 2. Many of them had figured out in the early 1990s that simply working for foreign companies would make Chinese cheap labourers forever. So they started to build their own factories and produce small things they could finance locally—such as clothing, shoes, toys and all sorts of small commodities.

By the early 2000s, in pretty much every major city in China, you could find a marketplace called a 'Yiwu small commodity market' (Yiwu is a small town near Wenzhou, where most of the manufacturing was going on). The marketplace, which sometimes takes up several floors in a mall, sells all kinds of household products. These markets are like the two-dollar Chinese shops you can find in Sydney only much bigger, with hundreds of individual shops.

While some Wenzhou people were busy selling what they made in the domestic market, many others travelled the world to sell their products. They began to build their own brands and learned quickly how to break into major business channels such as the supermarkets and department stores. These people made their money honestly and diligently.

Many of the business owners were previously employees of foreign- or Hong Kong–owned factories. They had learned the production processes through working in them. I am not going to deny there were some dodgy ones who had no respect for intellectual property (IP) and stole designs or brands directly. From the mid 1990s, the Silk Street Market in Beijing was a popular destination for foreign travellers to China. The tourists did not go there to buy silk or other traditional products; they went to buy cheap counterfeit luxury goods such as LV or Chanel bags. Some Chinese counterfeit factories made them so well that even experts could not tell the difference. Some of the fake bags were actually made by the very contract factories that produced the original bags.

It is not a proud history for the Chinese, especially for my generation of educated people, who understand the importance of intellectual property. But back in the late 1990s there were too many poor and undereducated people in China. The IP laws were dysfunctional. More interestingly, there were just so many customers (in particular, foreign customers) willing to buy those products. Most Chinese people actually had no interest in the products themselves, because they were not familiar with the brands and could not understand why even counterfeit versions could sell for hundreds of yuan.

Later, when they got rich and began to purchase luxury goods, it was an embarrassment to be found to have purchased counterfeit versions. They wanted the real thing because they were paying real money. People who purchased and used the fake items were often despised. When China joined the WTO, the government closed lots of illegal businesses in the Silk Street Market and many other markets in China that sold counterfeit products.

I am sure counterfeit products are still being made and sold in China, but certainly not publicly and not on the scale they used to be. People do get arrested and charged for breaking IP laws. All the luxury brands have opened their own retail stores in major cities such as Beijing and Shanghai and, to the surprise of many, the luxury brands did so well that China became a major market for these brands. Many Chinese tourists go to Europe or Australia to purchase luxury goods because the taxes there are lower than in China, or sometimes the exchange rate works in favour of the Chinese consumer.

Most luxury goods for the Chinese consumer need to meet just one criterion to qualify as a luxury — the goods should *not* have been made in China; this is especially important for cosmetics, clothing and leather products. So rich people in China give their hard-earned cash obtained from selling made-in-China products to overseas companies that make not-made-in-China products. Which is quite ironic, I think.

THE EVOLVING IT INDUSTRY IN CHINA

When I was in high school in Beijing, there was an interesting place called Zhongguancun, where students often went to buy pirated CDs. I lived on the east side of Beijing and had to ride my bike for 40 minutes from my home to Zhongguancun, which was located on the other side of Beijing. You could find a great variety of CDs there, including software, games, movies and even pornography.

There were many reasons why the Chinese bought pirated CDs in China. Cost was important, of course. A Chinese-version Microsoft Windows 95 pack cost over 1000 yuan in 1997. No one except big companies could afford to buy it at that price. But you could get it for just 10 yuan at Zhongguancun, so you could install Windows on your own computers and learn how to use it. It was the same with Word, Excel and Photoshop.

Actually, many people believed Microsoft's strategy was to allow piracy of its software in China, so Chinese people would become familiar with their software and system, rather than with what was offered by Apple. If that was Bill Gates's strategy, I am certain it worked out really well. Almost no one of my generation used Apple computers, unless they only did graphic design work. The Chinese became so familiar with Internet Explorer that even today most Chinese government websites and bank websites work only in IE, rather than in Chrome or Firefox.

Returning to the main topic of how the Chinese became so rich, a huge amount of money was made from information technology, through manufacturing and selling of computers, software development, the internet, and mobile phones and applications.

I say in chapter 2 that China was more than a hundred years behind the United States in residential plumbing, but only a few years behind in IT. During my childhood, all computers were imported—from the US or Japan for example. After these foreign companies began setting up factories in China, China developed its own brand called Legend, later changing its name to Lenovo when it acquired the personal computer business from IBM. Soon we saw the growth of more and more local brands for manufacturing computers.

When I was in high school, even before the landline was common in Chinese homes, the telecom companies started building broadband in major cities. Today China is the biggest market for information technology, with 700 million desktop internet and mobile internet users (more half of the population). A great many of these users had never previously used a computer but went directly to mobile internet.

So, unlike my generation of Chinese, who needed to take a 40-minute bike ride to buy cheap CDs, the younger generation can download everything directly. After the Chinese government closed down the Zhongguancun pirated-CD market when it joined the WTO, piracy moved online through BT download, a new technology that helped people to share large media and other computer files. It was popular for a few years before being blocked by the government.

A few years ago, when Youku (the Chinese version of YouTube) became popular in China, there was no longer any need even to download; you could watch anything directly and instantly on computers and mobile phones. The website owners could effectively control the distribution of media and start collecting royalties for the content owners. This happened with software manufacturers too, when traditional CD distribution gave way to online downloads with monthly or annual subscriptions.

These changes made piracy much harder. But what changed everything in China was the growth in household income and reduction in software prices. Compared with 10 years ago, piracy lost its market because it became both too much trouble and simply unnecessary to more and more Chinese, who could afford to pay for the technology they needed and not break the law.

While the Chinese IT hardware and software industries have been open to the rest of the world from the very beginning, access to the internet is another story. Before it became popular in China, the internet was free just as it was in most of the world. But after the political event in 1999, the Chinese government started to recognise the great potential of the internet as a tool for political propaganda and the need to control it.

While I was in university between 2000 and 2004, the Great Firewall of China (GFW) was still quite basic. It could block only a few selected websites that obviously had political views different from those of the Chinese government. By the time I returned to China in 2010, the GFW had pretty much transformed China's internet into an intranet (a local area network). In 2010 Google shut down its search engine services to China because it did not want to conform to the censorship requirements of the Chinese government. This was not a very smart move on Google's part, in my opinion. I would rather have a cut-down version of Google than Baidu.

Because the internet in China was fairly insulated from the rest of the world, and yet the number of users was huge, the market spawned a great number of giant Chinese internet companies. You can find Alibaba, which focuses on online trading and also runs the Taobao, the Chinese version of eBay. And you can find Tencent, which owns QQ and WeChat, which have dominated the Chinese market for online communication. Both companies are competing to dominate the Chinese market for mobile-based payments. There is a Chinese version of Twitter (Weibo) and a Chinese version of Uber (Didi). There is a Chinese equivalent of virtually everything that exists outside the GFW.

China has the technology and the market to maintain its own internet. The internet also generated many opportunities to make money. If you subscribe to the Chinese social media, almost every day you will see news stories of someone who got rich overnight by creating a new website or app. Some of these stories are marketing stunts, but most of them are real, and the stories of Chinese becoming wealthy through information technology go on and on. Internet technology helps account for a significant proportion of the Chinese wealth seen by the rest of the world.

THE HIDDEN COSTS OF MONETARY WEALTH

When I returned to Beijing from Sydney in 2010, the flight landed at Beijing's new airport late at night. The sky was dark but the city was bright. From the sky, I could see a semi-transparent dome over the city. I would not be sure of what that was until five years later when a former CCTV journalist, Chai Jing, released her self-financed Chinese documentary film *Under the Dome*. The documentary talked about air pollution in China, in particular in major cities on the eastern coast. Suddenly I realised it was the same dome I had seen from the plane.

So I knew it had actually been there for a while. Millions of people fly over the dome and see it every day. Hundreds of millions of people, including government officials, have lived under the dome of air pollution every day, and yet it took many years for the government to address the issue. That started me thinking about how the Chinese had been probably too busy making money and had simply ignored the hidden costs of economic development. It also made me wonder about the other hidden costs behind the economic miracle of China.

The one-child policy is a big one. As I describe at the beginning of the book, my parents' generation spent most of their time and energy on working and business that greatly boosted the country's GDP. They sacrificed family time because in their minds it was more important to earn money and improve the material living conditions of the family than to spend lots of time with their children. By the time they had more money in their pockets, the country had already experienced big changes, and the people discovered the world outside China and the opportunities it offered. So it was important for them to continue their work so they could either go overseas themselves or, more often, send their children.

Those who never left China and never sent their children overseas had to work hard just to keep up with inflation. A friend told me a story about her father. In the 1990s he made 100 000 Chinese yuan in business and decided on early retirement. In China back then that was a lot of money, with a purchasing power equivalent to $10 million today. If I had that kind of money, I would not hesitate to retire early. But in just a few years his assets had depreciated from a huge fortune to a modest sum that was barely enough to cover his daughter's university education. So he had to come out of retirement and go back to work again.

This generation had the freedom to work whenever they wanted to. And in the city it was common for both parents to work long hours. They usually had only one child to raise; and the grandparents were very helpful, assuming a responsibility to help raise their grandchildren. This gave young parents in China a lot more time to focus on their career and business. The loss of valuable family time could have very negative consequences, however.

When I moved to Beijing in 1997 to join my parents for the first time since 1983, a friend of my father's had a son the same age as me who hanged himself at home. Separated from his parents for many years, he had a background quite similar to mine. When he moved to Beijing to join his parents, apparently something went badly wrong and he decided to end his life. He wasn't alone in facing such problems. When I was 17, I had moments of great depression when I could have done something stupid.

Chinese parents at that time had a single-minded focus on their career and the accumulation of monetary wealth. They spent little time and energy on their children's general health, let alone their mental health. But I cannot really blame them. They had little time for their own physical and mental health either. They probably suffered more ill health than their peers in Australia through lack of exercise and the heavy pollution of air, water and soil. All these hidden costs added and continue to add to their (and their children's) medical bills.

The government might not have realised the magnitude of these hidden costs at first, but it sure learned and improved on that front. Hu Jintao was the Chinese president from 2003 to 2013. His 'Scientific Outlook on Development' was a Chinese version of sustainable development theory. The communist leadership has realised that a sole focus on the economy—where the Chinese reform had started from 1978—will no longer work in twenty-first century China. The Chinese people need more than money for a happy life. The growing middle class in China may not want another revolution, but they certainly want a better-regulated society so their rights are better protected. In other words, they want to be 'citizens' rather than just 'civilians'.

These new citizens are great at using social media to spread their opinions and bring together like-minded people. They do not use Facebook but focus only on the social media available inside China such as Weibo or WeChat. Some of them have millions of followers, potentially enough to start a revolution. But they are smart enough not to oppose the government and rather to work with it in a peaceful way.

Their influence has forced the government, in particular at the local level, to act more responsibly, for example when considering tearing down a heritage building or imposing a new tax. Incidents around social issues such as pollution or police violence can find their way onto social media and spread to millions of people in minutes. People who might feel street demonstrations are too risky do not hesitate to retweet and share negative news on local government.

Bad news from social media soon catches the attention of the mainstream media, including state-owned media. Local governments have to correct their errors quickly or their officials could land in big trouble. This process is playing a growing role in reducing or at least controlling some of the hidden costs that are threatening China's economic growth. However, the damage that has already been done to the environment and society will probably take the Chinese another 20 to 30 years to repair.

THE CONCENTRATION OF WEALTH

The final and most important reason there are so many rich Chinese in the world is that monetary wealth is highly concentrated. Whatever definition you use, the rich Chinese are a tiny minority of the country. In 2013 China's GDP per capita was US$6800, one-tenth of Australia's (US$67 458). So if Australians are 10 times richer on average than Chinese, why do the Chinese buyers of properties and luxury goods in Australia appear to be so rich? This has to do with how the Chinese like to spend their money but, more importantly, with the way income is distributed among the Chinese people.

A report by Peking University put the Gini coefficient for China in 2014 at 0.73 (which indicates a highly unequal distribution). About 1 per cent of Chinese families own about one-third of the country's total wealth, while 25 per cent of families at the bottom of society hold only 1 per cent of the total social wealth. Other studies present somewhat different figures, but they all point to the same conclusion: a very small percentage of super-rich Chinese families hold a significant proportion of the social wealth, mostly in the form of cash and real estate. Let's say only 1 per cent of Chinese are super rich. Given a population of 1.38 billion, that still indicates 13.8 million super-rich Chinese—equivalent to more than half the entire Australian population.

There are a few explanations for the unequal distribution of wealth in China. First and foremost is the unequal distribution between the cities and rural areas. When I was young, people talked about the 'price scissors' when referring to the unfair distribution of income between primary-industry and secondary-industry workers in China. The government maintained strong price controls on agricultural products and intentionally set low prices for all the major agricultural products, such as rice and wheat.

As a result, food remained cheap for many decades. The cheap food supply to the city helped fund the growth of secondary-industry workers. This is the fundamental reason why China could keep labour costs down over the past 30 years and became the world's factory. The rural population had much more limited opportunities for education and work. Because of the low income in rural areas, the younger people had to leave home to find work in the city. More and more poor farmers became industrial workers.

This in turn drove the population growth in the cities and urbanisation. Some of the rural workers made their living and settled in the city permanently; many had to return home when they grew older and became unfit for work in the factories. Some took home nothing but diseases such as lung cancer from asbestos pollution contracted while building high-rise properties in the city. The medical insurance system in China covers only certain workers in the city; it does not cover people in rural areas or even city-based workers with a rural background. Once they get sick, they become extremely poor. It is as though they have worked their whole life for nothing.

The difference between the cities and the villages is extreme in terms of the concentration of wealth. Half of China's rural population are considered to be very poor. There are exceptions of course; in rare cases, rural people can be richer than city people, especially when the local land is valuable.

Another fault line for wealth distribution is between the eastern coastal cities and the inland cities. Their geographical advantage has meant that east coast cities such as Beijing, Shanghai and Guangzhou have historically had greater access to foreign investment and international trade. They also have much bigger populations. More than 90 per cent of the population lives in the east of the country. Most of the education, business and social resources are concentrated on the east coast. People who live in the west simply have a lot less opportunity. And with the rise of the mega-cities in China, more and more people from the west are moving towards the east, further compounding the imbalance.

The unfair distribution of wealth is quite normal in a country in its early stages of industrialisation. What is not normal is how it stands today compared with 30 years ago, when the Gini coefficient in the country was, theoretically at least, zero (no one owned anything). What makes it more incredible is that this happened under the banner of Communism, which is supposed to bring about financial equality.

The inequality is likely to cause a myriad social problems, including political instability. When I talked to some older friends about what they thought had been the reason for the 1989 event, many of them believed it had been more about inequality than democracy. When Deng Xiaoping encouraged capitalist-style reforms in China, some people became rich, which angered others who probably felt better when everyone was equally poor.

When there was more money around, corruption (which had pretty much disappeared during the Cultural Revolution) made a big comeback. Some government officials accumulated huge wealth from accepting bribes and from selling public resources. The fight for democracy was in fact a fight for economic justice. Although in the past 30 years the Chinese people have come to accept that some inequality is inevitable, the widening gap may one day trigger another revolution.

Many wealthy people in China, whether their fortune was earned through hard work or collected from bribes, have opted to move their family wealth to a safer country. Since the late 1990s, the rich Chinese have never stopped sending their money overseas. For many years there was little control over the outflow of capital from China through underground banks (most likely because government officials were using these channels to send out their own money). In late 2015 the government suddenly tightened this outflow and it has since taken down many underground banks operating in China.

This has made it a lot harder for the Chinese to send their money overseas to fund the purchase of properties. Nevertheless, where there is a will there is always a way. The more controls the government puts in place, the more worried the rich in China will become. I would not be surprised to see even more funds coming out of China in the next few years, especially if the Chinese economy does not perform as well as it has over the past three decades.

CHAPTER SUMMARY

- From one of the world's poorest developing countries to the world's second largest economy, China has become rich through 30 years of real economic growth.

- An important part of this growth has been from exporting manufactured goods to the rest of the world.

- The IT hardware and software industries have played a significant role, first through allowing foreign corporations to set up assembly plants in China, then through developing their own brands.

- The hidden costs behind the economic miracle include the one-child policy and the sacrifice of family made by the boomer generation and environmental degradation (air, water and soil pollution) triggering widespread ill health and rising medical costs.

- Wealth is highly concentrated, with the richest 1 per cent owning one-third of China's total wealth. Unequal distribution of resources between cities and rural areas, and east and west, is a likely source of future instability.

中华人民共和国
PEOPLE'S REPUBLIC OF CHINA
DEPARTURE
NOV 18 2011
BEIJING

CHAPTER 7

THE CHINESE CONSUMER

CHINESE PROPERTY OBSESSION

The different generations of new Chinese have had distinctively different experiences of property purchasing. My parents' generation did not have to purchase any property. Under the old planned-economy system, housing was 'allocated' by the state. I am not familiar with the system because it was abolished in 1994, but the principle was that the state would build properties based on the plan, then these properties would be allocated based on need. For example, a married couple would normally be given priority over a younger single person in the allocation of a property.

There were (almost) no rich people, and no one was allowed to have more living space than they needed. On the other hand, even the poorest people would have a place to live. The big courtyard where I had lived when I was in Suzhou had belonged to a member of the 'landlord class', exploiters of the working-class people, so the property had to be returned to the working poor in the city.

But this free public housing was cramped. According to official Chinese statistics, the per capita living area in Chinese cities in 1978 was just 6.3 square metres. I can confirm this figure from personal experience, as until early 1990 I lived in a room that was probably below-average size. For most adults, the dream was to work in the government- or state-owned corporations and factories, which would ensure they were allocated a property in the near future. But before long the government figured out that the allocation policy was unsustainable, given the rapid population growth over the decades.

When the babies became adults and married, they needed space for their own kids. The cheap labourers flocking in from the rural areas also needed living space, but they were not included in the city's housing plan. As the country transitioned from a planned to a market economy, properties became commodities like anything else. So in 1994 the old system was abolished, and those who had not been allocated a property before 1994 were expected to buy their own.

So the Gen X Chinese, born during the Cultural Revolution, were the first generation of new Chinese that had to purchase their home. The way property is purchased in a Chinese city is very different from how it is purchased in Australia.

First, property ownership itself is quite different. All land in all the cities in China is owned by the state, and citizens can acquire property by leasehold for 70 years (sometimes less than 70 years). This is similar to property in Canberra, all of which is based on a 99-year lease.

The land and the property on top of the land are separate things. The building can be individually or jointly owned by property purchasers. So what happens after 70 years when the lease to the land expires? Does the owner of the property have to renew the lease for another 70 years? I don't know the answer, and neither do most Chinese. Purchase of leasehold land became possible only in 1978. I expect the first legal cases regarding leasehold land renewal will not happen until around

2048. It is simply too far in the future for people to worry about now.

Second, properties are rarely individually priced but are most often priced by the square metre. For example, the average price per square metre in Beijing in 2016 was above 50 000 yuan. This puts the cost of a 100-square-metre, three-bedroom apartment in Beijing at 5 million yuan, or roughly $1 million. So the typical Chinese buyer coming from Beijing to Sydney and seeing so many properties priced below $1 million, with 700 or 800 square metres of permanent land and four or five bedrooms, saw great buying opportunities.

And for my generation of new Chinese, who do not own property in Beijing or Shanghai, it is even harder to work and purchase our own property there than in Australia. This helps explain why large numbers of Chinese buyers (both overseas investors and local families) have pushed property prices up here.

Lastly, the property rental market in China is largely underdeveloped. The cost of letting out property is high, and the return is low. A 2014 news article showed the average rent per square metre in Beijing was just 62.3 yuan. This meant that the annual rental return in Beijing was probably just 1.5 per cent. Most families that owned more than one property would rather keep the property empty than let it out, because the cost of maintenance could exceed the rental income.

By comparison, the 3 to 5 per cent gross rental return in Australia is definitely very attractive, not to mention the huge capital gains Australia has seen since 2012. So, unless the government places even stricter rules on foreign property investors, nothing is going to stop the Chinese from buying up Australian properties. The opportunity is simply too good to miss.

For a typical Chinese family living in Sydney, their traditional family culture and structure mean one property is simply not enough. When I look at my friends who are originally from China, they all had their mother or mother-in-law living with them when their first child was born in Australia. Chinese grandparents feel an obligation to help raise their grandchildren. But living together with their grown-up children and their children's spouses does often raise tensions. The two generations of Chinese do not have much in common. In the eyes of their children, who have been educated in a western culture, Chinese parents are mostly seen as domineering and demanding. So they will buy or rent a separate property for their parents, if they can afford to.

In most cases, the grandparents actually have enough savings to purchase the properties themselves. Even if they are not permanent residents, they do not mind purchasing the properties in their child's name to avoid stamp duty penalties aimed at overseas property purchasers. As gifts are not taxed in Australia, the new stamp duty policy to stop overseas investors is useless against Chinese investors who have children in Australia who are already permanent residents or citizens.

BUYING FACE – TO FULFIL A PROMISE

Property is probably the primary item on which the Chinese have spent their money in recent years in both China and Australia. At the same time, they have made significant outlays on education, holidays, luxury goods, antiques, food and beverage. There is an intrinsic value to the things people buy, of course, but there is also a special value for the Chinese that most westerners do not understand — the value of 'face' embedded in these acquisitions.

There are quite a few thoroughly researched and well-written articles on the internet that can tell you about this concept and how to use it to your advantage. I have my own theory about the concept of 'face'. In my view, face to the Chinese is about *promise*, which can be both written down and implied.

When the world was hit by the global financial crisis (GFC) in 2008, China launched a 4 trillion yuan (about US$586 billion) economic stimulus program. Many economists, both outside and inside China, dismissed the program as a 'face project', like so many other such initiatives in China. A 'face project' is a program that offers no substance or long-term effectiveness, but is executed simply to make someone look good. To me, this program aimed to fulfil an implied promise from government to people that China would keep growing at a faster rate than the world average. And, by measurable GDP, the government fulfilled this promise for a few years after the GFC.

But those critics were probably right too. Nine years after the GFC, excessive infrastructure and output capacity fuelled by the 4 trillion yuan stimulus package has meant that the Chinese economy today faces more uncertainty than it did during the crisis. Many people believe that China is heading towards a long-term recession. But for the sake of not 'losing face', even recession has a different name in China. It is called 'the new normal'.

The repeated mention of the new normal in the state-owned media is an effort to establish a new promise between the government and the people. The old promise is no longer sustainable. The Chinese economy will not continue to grow as it has in the past 30 years. This has to be accepted by its own people first. Under the new normal, the economy will remain under stress for a long time, and more funds will leave China as people seek profits elsewhere in the world.

Government-controlled funds are investing in surrounding countries through the 'belt and road' initiative and the Asian Infrastructure Investment Bank (AIIB). Both are great initiatives to make better use of China's US$3 trillion foreign exchange reserve and to transfer China's excess production capacity to countries that still have cheap labour. Equally important, stronger economic and political influence in the world would help the Chinese government to 'gain face'. Here the face comes with another important implied promise the government has made to its own people and to the rest of the world—that China has become a responsible big country. And as a responsible big country, China should help its poor neighbours to develop their economies.

In spite of the government's efforts and strict foreign currency controls, a large number of businesses are investing overseas. Some are purchasing strategically important businesses in agriculture and healthcare because, with its large and ageing population, these are industries that will continue to boom in China over the next few decades. Some are investing for more short-term returns, such as in real estate development.

Here is a story to illustrate the concept of 'face'. One of China's largest state-owned property development companies purchased an old building in the Sydney CBD and planned to build a 235-metre-high residential tower in the heart of Sydney. The project was sold out at launch in 2014, but because of disputes with the builder and the local council, construction work did not start until 2016. The best estimate is that it will not be completed until 2019 or 2020. Some investors might worry that the project will never be completed. Not so the Chinese buyers. They know this is a face project for one of the largest state-owned companies in China. The project may result in big financial losses due to the delays, but the company will maintain their high standards. They can afford the financial loss, but they cannot afford a loss of face.

My mother-in-law (along with many other people living in China) worries a great deal about China's 'red envelope' culture. People are expected to send a red envelope on all important occasions, such as weddings, birthdays or even funerals (the envelope would be white in this case), to classmates, bosses, colleagues, relatives, suppliers, customers, and sometimes neighbours and their immediate families. The red envelope can range from several hundred yuan to over a thousand yuan, depending on the occasion and relationship. This 'gesture' is expected to maintain normal social relationships. There is no law or formal agreement for people to do this; it is just an implied social promise that every Chinese recognises.

My mother-in-law could not escape this promise even when she was physically outside China. Her former colleagues (she retired 10 years ago) would send her a message saying that someone's daughter had just got married and a 500-yuan 'red envelope' had been sent to them on my mother-in-law's behalf. Because she was not in China, she could repay the 500 yuan later when she returned. And if my mother-in-law said no, she would lose face for breaking this implicit promise and would be criticised by all her former colleagues.

There are plenty of implied promises in China to trigger the gaining or loss of face. When we visit someone, it is important to bring a gift. Visiting someone without a gift will lead to a breach of the social contract and therefore a loss of face. The more valuable the gift is (although it needs to be within a reasonable range), the better we fulfil the promise and gain face. Most Chinese also implicitly promise they will meet people's expectations in terms of their physical appearance. When you become rich it is important to wear an expensive watch and jewellery and carry a branded bag; otherwise you are failing people's expectations and breaking a social promise.

For the above reasons, luxury goods industries are doing extremely well in China—probably too well for a country with a per capita GDP of only US$6800. The concentration of wealth in a small group of Chinese is one important reason, but even ordinary Chinese need to purchase luxury goods for gifts in order not to lose face in a social situation.

Finally, most Chinese who come to Australia as tourists have made an implied promise to their relatives and friends that they will bring home gifts for them. For this reason they sometimes spend more time shopping for gifts than actually enjoying the places they visit. More than one tourist gift shop specifically for Chinese has opened on every street in Chinatown as well as in every suburb with a high density of Chinese residents in Sydney.

Some products are really overpriced in these shops, but that does not matter greatly to the customers, because a high and conspicuous price tag shows their family and friends how much they have spent. Finally, for some Chinese, gifts are more about 'face value' than actual value.

AIM FOR THE FUTURE

Compared with typical westerners, the Chinese are very future oriented. Because of this, they take a long-term approach when spending money. This is particularly true for older people. After experiencing the Great Famine, my parents' generation built the habit of saving for the future—saving food, saving money, saving everything. The most penny-pinching ones will 'save' ketchup and sugar sachets from McDonald's restaurants. In most public toilets in China, toilet rolls are not provided because some people will actually take them home to save money.

Most of the younger generation have moved on from these behaviours and probably despise their parents for being too thrifty. Having never suffered poverty and hunger as their parents did, they don't really care about saving.

The habit of saving is closely linked to the pattern of how the older generation spend their money. Extravagant spending for today is disapproved of. Spending for the future, on the other hand, is encouraged—it is called investment. One extremely important form of investment is education. Since ancient times, ordinary Chinese families have supported their children's studies—the more advanced the better.

Under the traditional Confucian education system, students devoted much of their time to studying classical literature, philosophy and etiquette. Good students could sit the provincial exams, with the best progressing to the national exams. The top national graduates would be summoned to the palace to be tested by the emperor himself. Achieving great results in national and palace exams would guarantee the student's future in China's civil service bureaucracy. A lucky and handsome one might even get a chance to marry a princess and join the royal family.

For Chinese parents of old, their children's exam results meant everything. Good results all but guaranteed career success in the world. Unfortunately this is no longer true, in either China or Australia. But when it comes to investing in the future of their offspring, the Chinese still have no hesitation in spending very large sums of money.

Indeed, the Chinese do not hesitate to invest in anything they believe to be of future value, even when, as in many cases, the investment decision is less than rational. Jack Ma (founder of Alibaba) recently pointed to a difference between Chinese and Americans: the Chinese as consumers are rational, but as investors are sensual; the Americans as consumers are sensual, but as investors are rational. I do not know how true the American part is, but he is definitely right about the Chinese part, even for the Chinese who have been living in Australia for more than a decade.

For example, most Chinese would never engage a financial planner. (I know I never have, and neither have most of the Chinese I know in Sydney.) They do not believe they need a professional to plan their investments, seeing financial planners as no more than salespeople who will push insurance and other unwanted financial products. They would rely on an article written by a nobody on WeChat or Weibo for investment advice rather than pay a professional to work out a plan for them.

In 2014, the *Oxford Dictionary* added a new term to its collection: 'Chinese Dama'. It describes undereducated middle-aged investors (mostly females, because it is they who have normally controlled the family finances since the Cultural Revolution). Perhaps a Chinese equivalent of western mum-and-dad investors, they have little knowledge of risk but follow the market sensually, and they invest heavily in certain financial products.

In late 2012 it was gold, then the gold price crashed. In 2015 it was the share market, then the share market crashed. It is unfortunate that the Dama make so many impulsive investment decisions in China. The better-educated younger Chinese actually have never had much in the way of savings to invest. Most of them have only a heavy mortgage debt from purchasing increasingly expensive properties.

By 2016 the Chinese economy was not doing well. The worse the economy is, the more reluctant people are to spend. In my hometown, Qitaihe, retail was in a great recession brought on by population outflow and the declining price of coal ore — the city's only industry. A friend from Qitaihe told me the newly opened shopping centre (a product of the counter-GFC stimulus package) almost never had customers. All the new businesses such as restaurants and fashion shops opened for a few weeks then promptly went out of business. All but one, that is.

One shop that sold Buddhist and other religious ritual products did really well. It was the only shop that stayed open in the new shopping centre, even in the terrible economic conditions. That surprised me initially, but when I thought about it, it really made sense. In the tough economy, all the young people had to leave their hometown to look for opportunities in big cities such as Harbin (the capital of the province) or Beijing, which is why most retail businesses could not survive. But for many reasons the older people could not leave the city, and they were a lot more superstitious than the younger people. Without many other outlets, they would spend on praying to the Buddha for a better next life. When they could see no other future, it was probably the only kind they could invest in.

The old generation of Chinese likes to invest for the future. They also like saving. The national private savings for China has been high for many years, which has led to 'insufficient domestic consumption', according to some economists. In reality, it is not that the Chinese do not want to consume, but that they cannot afford to spend too much today when the future holds such great uncertainties.

The country has a really low coverage of medical insurance and retirement pension. Unemployment insurance is next to nonexistent. People living in China do not have the certainty of social benefits they can rely on, as in Australia and other developed countries. It is therefore important for everyone to have savings. To keep the savings safe, and to avoid financial loss from risky investment and natural depreciation, it makes sense to move them to a safe, socially stable country such as Australia.

HOW TO SELL TO THE CHINESE

In the big, fast-moving consumer goods company my wife works for, management devotes a lot of energy to their China strategy. Last year one of their products, a mosquito repellent for children, sold really well in China through *Daigous* (Chinese shopping agents). This year they produced more of the same product specifically for the Chinese market, and thoughtfully added labels with Chinese information. To their great surprise, the product did not sell as well.

The marketing department could not understand why. They consulted an external expert, who came up with an explanation that I could have given them for free: it was a mistake to put a Chinese label on their product. The Chinese wanted that company's products *because* they were Australian made. They believed that Australian products were safe, especially products for children (such as baby formula).

To look like a good Australian product, there should have been no Chinese label at all. When they saw the Chinese label, consumers were simply less interested in buying. In the same way, when Australians are looking to buy an expensive French perfume, they prefer to see labelling and packaging in French only. If it is printed in English, they may feel less drawn to the product.

Inside China, some Chinese companies make products with all-English packaging and market them as foreign brands. This is a very popular technique in the second- and third-tier cities in China. Consumers in these cities have relatively less experience of shopping overseas, and the leading foreign brands have yet to reach their shopping centres. So in these places you may find Chinese burger shops looking like McDonald's and fried chicken outlets looking like KFC, along with many 'European' fashion brands you will never find in Europe.

Surprisingly, this dodgy strategy has worked pretty well in these cities. This success rests on the widespread perception that foreign products are of higher quality than locally made products. And this applies not just to things made in developed countries, but also to products from Thailand or Vietnam. In recent years, the increasingly transparent social media have made the Chinese aware of the number of unsafe or low-quality products manufactured inside the country, so many foreign products have become popular (despite being more expensive) simply because they are not made in China. Which all helps to explain why Zhen's company's marketing plan of using Chinese labelling backfired.

Language is no longer a barrier for Chinese shopping around the world. Take my mother, for instance. She speaks little English, but she has no trouble shopping in Sydney, even in a shop where no one speaks Chinese. Once she went to a shop to buy a watch. She just used universal body language to tell the shop assistant which one she was interested in. Then she started negotiating the price with the shop assistant, who did not speak Chinese at all.

All my mother could say was 'yes', 'no', 'okay', 'thank you' and 'goodbye'. She took out her calculator and keyed in the price she was willing to offer. The shop assistant did not agree and put in a different number, then she bargained back. After a few rounds, my mum said 'okay' and happily bought the watch. With her Union Pay card (the Chinese equivalent to Visa or MasterCard), she could pay for the watch in either US dollars or Chinese yuan from her Chinese bank account. And she would receive an instant SMS notification from her bank when the purchase was complete. Of course, when she meets someone in a shop who speaks Chinese, the conversation is longer and she does a lot more haggling.

I find my mother to be a very typical Chinese consumer of her generation. Researching how she purchases products has given me a pretty good snapshot of how other Chinese do their buying. For example, my mother never purchased insurance before taking me on an airplane when I was a child. Her explanation was simple: If something happened to the plane, the insurance compensation would be useless to her or to me. It is very unlikely that anyone would survive an air catastrophe; the chances are so small that it can safely be ignored. I actually agree with her on this.

One year when I was travelling with her she surprised me by announcing we were both insured. I asked her why she had bought the insurance. She said she did not buy it—it was free. All she had to do was invest a certain amount of money (in the bank) in a special (probably risky) product with a variable return, and the bank provided free travel insurance to her and her family. So it was 'free'! I knew very well it was not free, but that I would probably fall for the same stunt. The Chinese banks are smart. When they bundle a normally unpopular product as a freebie with an 'investment', they can sell it to anyone, including my very economical mother.

I found the consumer behaviour of the younger generation of Chinese was not that different from the younger generation of Australians. They might be using different social media, but they follow a similar pattern when making purchases. For example, my friend Joyce (a 90-hou born in 1993) told me she buys all her clothes online because she can make purchase decisions without anyone else's help.

This is something my (80-hou) generation would not do. We trust physical shops more than online shops. And we prefer to try clothes on than just see them on models. I know I will never look the same as the models online. But apparently Joyce can picture the item better on the models than on herself, and can save herself the trouble visiting the shop to try it on.

I am very sure that many of the younger generation of Australians would agree with her. I recently got to know a successful entrepreneur in Sydney, the founder of online retail brand Showpo. Jane Lu markets all her clothes online through Facebook and Instagram, and she does much better than the big retail players in attracting customers between the ages of 16 and 29.

The traditional department stores operated by and for the older generation never believed it would be possible to sell millions of dollars' worth of clothes per month online, but the younger people made it happen. The lesson I took from this was that I should no longer trust myself and my own preferences when advising clients on how to sell to the Chinese. Rather, I needed to find out more about the actual market they wanted to target, especially if it was the younger generation.

CHAPTER SUMMARY

- With the shift from planned economy to market economy, the Gen X Chinese became the first generation of new Chinese that had to purchase their home.

- The economic boom saw property values skyrocket, especially in the big cities, which helps explain why overseas Chinese buyers have pushed up property prices in Australia.

- For Chinese people, significant acquisitions have an embedded value beyond the intrinsic called 'face' value, which implies a promise.

- New Chinese are future oriented. They place a high value on saving and investment for the future, whether in their children's education or in property in a more socially stable country such as Australia.

- When selling to the Chinese, as to any other market, find out more about the specific target market, especially if it is the younger generation.

CHAPTER 8

NEW CHINESE IN THE WORKFORCE

THE NEW CHINESE GRADUATES

Like many international students from China, when I graduated from Macquarie University with a master's degree in accounting and finance in 2007, I was not very confident I would get a good accounting job in Australia. My goal was a graduate role in a big company — one of the Big Four accounting firms or banks, or any ASX-listed company or multinational subsidiary. I had heard it was pretty hard for someone from China, unless the person was born in Australia or had come while really young. Spoken English was a big barrier for those who arrived at a mature age, as I did. Many of my classmates did not even bother trying. I decided to give it a go anyway.

I remember I had this big folder containing information on all the graduate programs offered by these big companies. There were about a hundred companies on my list. Applying for a graduate role was a very painful process. For every company, I had to fill out lengthy application forms, then I had to take online tests on mathematics and verbal reasoning. After all this work, I got just 10 calls for a telephone interview. I survived a few of those but was rejected in most of the face-to-face interviews that followed. Three companies, Qantas, ANZ and Shell, invited me to a final round of group assessment. This meant completing a project with a team of graduates who were exclusively local Australians or Australian-born Asians.

I did plenty of preparation beforehand, but still I found I could hardly follow their ideas or speak up intelligently in such an intense environment. I had tried hard and spent hundreds of hours on it, but I eventually failed all the applications. I simply could not get into a big company through the graduate channel in 2007.

It came as no surprise to me. Besides my poor spoken English, I also lacked work experience in the relevant field. All my fellow graduates were fresh in the area, but it was general life experience I fell short in. When they enrol for a master's degree, most Australians have already had at least a few years of work experience. But most students from China, even today, go straight from a bachelor's to a master's program before getting a chance to utilise what they have learned in a real workplace. And generally they have no idea what they should expect from a master's-level education. Even worse, they probably have no experience working in the real world—not even at McDonald's or Woolworths. Their parents, like mine, would have strongly discouraged them from doing any part-time work while they were at university, demanding they focus solely on their studies and achieving good grades.

Many of them never even participated in student unions or other voluntary roles because these would be seen as distractions by the parents who were funding their education. So, compared with their Australian peers, a typical graduate from China would have an impressive academic record but absolutely nothing else to show the recruiter of a big company—nothing to demonstrate their personal initiative or their teamwork aptitude, and certainly, given the reticence they had absorbed at school through the Doctrine of the Mean philosophy, nothing to demonstrate their communication skills.

It is difficult for students who have come through an educational system that does not encourage them to speak out or debate to do well in face-to-face interviews. Fortunately, I was not completely jobless. While I was interviewing for these hard-to-get graduate roles, I was already working part-time for a not-for-profit organisation called the Royal Volunteer Coastal Patrol. I worked as an accounts clerk doing reconciliations for its 26 divisions across Australia.

My interviewer for that job, Sharyn, played a big part in getting my accounting career started. She had been to China many times and had had good Chinese friends since childhood, so she was very open-minded and helpful. I still remember the interview. I arrived at her office nervous and tongue-tied, and she pretty much guided me through the entire interview. She was confident I could do the job and pretty much offered it to me on the spot. I started the following Monday.

As she had expected, I worked very hard to prove she had made the right choice. This is a common experience I hear of when I talk to employers in the accounting industry who have hired students with a Chinese background. They agree that these applicants are not good communicators and maybe not great team workers (they are reluctant to ask for help, and prefer to work things out for themselves so as not to 'lose face'), but they do not mind working longer hours (with or without extra pay) and they get things done. I suppose this is good enough for most entry-level bean-counter roles.

Many years later, when I joined one of the Big Four accounting firms in Sydney, I saw quite a few new Chinese working there too. All but one of them was hired as an experienced applicant rather than as a graduate. This confirmed what had caused me to fail in 2007: it was simply too difficult for a Chinese student who came to Australia at a mature age to get into the leading graduate programs. Not completely impossible, but extremely difficult.

This, in my opinion, is because when companies hire graduates, they focus mainly on communication and soft skills. Learning such skills is fairly uncomplicated for local graduates; it is much more difficult for international students who have not been here long. They can do the work; where they often fail is in the face-to-face interview and group assessment, where talking is more important than doing.

Once they have experience, though, the assessment criteria change. That is why partners of the Big Four firms have no problem hiring them as auditors. For small- and medium-sized companies with a less systematic graduate hiring process, the new Chinese have little trouble getting hired and perform well.

Most university lecturers in Australia recognised that Chinese international students were shy and reserved, but for years not much was done to address the issue. In 2013 I saw some positive changes. Through CPA Australia, I was invited to the University of Technology Sydney for a discussion with accounting education providers from all the major universities in Australia. Those lecturers who were responsible for developing and delivering accounting courses finally agreed that the accounting education system failed to address the needs of international students as far as communications and other soft skills were concerned.

We sat down together to try to develop some new subjects that would specifically address communication, teamwork and self-management. As an industry representative, and someone with experience as an international student, it was a pleasure to share my insights and exciting to see the positive changes generated by the forum. From recent conversations I have had with new accounting graduates, I can see that at least some universities in Australia have finally put these special elements in place for international students from the new China.

THE BAMBOO CEILING

One of the benefits of working as an auditor for a Big Four firm is that I got to visit a different company every two weeks. Over the past few years I have visited almost a hundred companies in different industries and at different locations in Sydney. There is probably only one thing they all have in common: you can always find one or more Chinese working there (often in the accounting department), most likely a new Chinese, aged 20 to 40, from mainland China.

I find it is easy to connect with them right away, and they are excited to know that I too am from mainland China. Having someone on the audit team who speaks their language (in more ways than one) makes communication easier for them. And because of this, I often get to hear interesting stories that other auditors are unlikely to pick up. A common theme is the bamboo ceiling in their company. They often complain to me about the difficulty they experience in climbing the corporate ladder, attributing their failure to win a promotion to racial discrimination.

The same stories cropped up in the Big Four accounting firms, too. The audit department I was in had a strong focus on energy, utilities and mining. Before the GFC these were popular industries to invest in for Chinese state-owned enterprises (SOEs). The firm had therefore set up a separate department to focus on that market, and had hired a great number of auditors with Chinese backgrounds to make it easier to communicate and work with these clients.

But soon after the GFC, especially after President Xi's anti-corruption campaign, Chinese SOE investment pretty much stopped. Their Australian subsidiaries were doing nothing. The strategic value of this audit department and all its Chinese employees had evaporated. Not surprisingly, in the following few years most auditors of Chinese background either were made redundant or resigned from the firm, and the department was merged with a bigger department. The bamboo ceiling was quite apparent in the firm. When they were no longer needed, and they knew they would never be made managers, most of my colleagues of Chinese background decided to leave.

These cases seem to support the notion of a bamboo ceiling. I bet some CEOs and many partners in the Big Four firms do not really understand the new Chinese, and therefore have doubts regarding their ability to perform in certain leadership roles. This is natural. There is a popular term nowadays called 'unconscious bias', which was often discussed in the Big Four firm where I worked.

However, I can also see clearly why some of the Chinese who are complaining should not be promoted as managers. They might be great auditors with strong technical skills, but a manager or partner in a big accounting firm needs a quite different skill set. And unfortunately the Chinese are often not big on these skills.

I am not about to try to teach the new Chinese how to break through the bamboo ceiling. There are already well-written books on the subject—by Jane Hyun and others—and many books in English and Chinese by successful corporate leaders of Asian background. Rather, I want to tell you more about the ceilings in China.

This is a true story about a family friend who had been an international student just like me. He had started his accounting career in a small company, had moved to a medium company, then landed a job in a multinational company's Sydney division.

About five years into his professional accounting career, he felt he had reached the bamboo ceiling of the company and would never be promoted to manager.

It was 2009 and his company was facing a downturn, and he faced the possibility of losing his job. So he decided to go back to China, convinced that, with his great qualifications and work experience, he would instantly be welcomed by a big company and would soon be promoted to manager, or even CFO. Surely he would be much better off than if he stayed in Australia, stuck in his current position. With that hope, he returned to China.

Then things got interesting. He did find a good company, the branch of a major bank based in Hong Kong, and he did get a good salary—pretty much on par with what he had been making in Australia. Everyone in the company was Chinese, so there was no bamboo ceiling to worry about. But he was worried. Despite the longer working hours and the excessive social networking necessary (usually involving lots of alcohol), which he hated, there were invisible ceilings everywhere.

With his great qualifications and work experience, he was given an enormous workload, but he could see no chance of promotion. To get promoted in this company, being hardworking and good at what you did counted for nothing. You needed to be the son or daughter of someone special who could bring a big deposit to the bank, or, even better, a borrower of huge sums of money from the bank. His family did not have those kinds of connections. However hard he worked, he would never get promoted. And his direct manager was not shy about telling him so directly.

So he decided to come back to Australia. He soon found a good job in a fast-moving consumer goods company. He stopped worrying about the bamboo ceiling and focused on his work in management accounting. He was duly promoted to analyst then senior analyst, which is an ideal role for someone who is technically strong in accounting but not yet ready to lead a team.

Last year he moved to a major drinks company and was made finance manager. When I asked him about his tips for breaking the bamboo ceiling, his reply was quite simple: 'Just be yourself and do what you do best.' To him, that was all he needed to create a great career and life in Australia. He could not get that in China, no matter how hard he worked. There may not be a bamboo ceiling in China, but there are all kinds of other invisible obstacles for ordinary Chinese like him or me.

THE ALCOHOL STORY

It is perfectly normal to have a couple of social drinks after work in Australia. Before 2010 I would not mind having a bottle of beer or a glass of wine with my colleagues on Friday afternoon. In 2010 I went back to China to work. When I returned to Australia in 2011, after my worst hangover experience in China, I decided never to touch alcohol again. Here is what happened.

It was New Year's Eve of 2010. Instead of being with my family or friends, I was with work colleagues at a branch of the Agriculture Bank of China. It was a social event involving the bank and the company I worked for, which was a major client of the bank for financing. There were two round tables of about 20 people, and about 20 bottles of Chinese alcohol on the tables. I knew it would be a tough night, but I did not foresee how badly it would go.

First, you need to know that Chinese alcohol is quite different from beer and wine; it is more like vodka. The stuff we had that night contained 38 per cent alcohol, as best I can recall (assuming my memory was not permanently damaged that night).

The dinner started at 7 pm, and after 9 pm my memory went blank. I felt like I was already asleep, and I had three dreams. In the first dream, I had my hands against a tree, and I was vomiting violently. In the second dream, I was holding a key and trying hard to find the hole to put it in. In the third dream, I jerked awake in the middle of the night and set an alarm clock.

It turned out that I had not been dreaming. When the alarm woke me at 8 the next morning I was home in bed. Evidently I had managed to open the door with my key, and I could still taste the vomit in my mouth. I was also completely naked. I had no idea if a co-worker had sent me home or even seen me safely undressed.

But there was no time to think about that. I suddenly remembered the reason for the 8 o'clock alarm: I had to catch the high-speed train from where I worked to Shanghai, then take a flight to Hunan to meet my wife's big family (most of them for the very first time). I quickly cleaned myself up and dressed. I hurriedly packed all the gifts and dragged my big suitcase to the train station.

The security guy almost stopped me going through when he saw I could hardly walk straight. I made it to the airport in Shanghai, though. And now I began to worry that they would not let me onto the plane. Happily, the flight was delayed, and by boarding time I could walk straight.

Once on board I could finally relax. I called my wife and told her everything was fine. But looking at the phone I saw I had called her the previous night at midnight and talked for about 20 minutes. I had no memory of that conversation! I had also sent a few messages to my parents, including some wrong Chinese characters, though nothing inappropriate, I was relieved to see.

When we landed in Hunan it was already dark. It was about 10 hours since I had woken up and I began to feel a pain in my hand, then I found scratches on my fingers, suggesting the tree in my dream had been all too real. I had not felt a thing all day, and now it was as though my skin and nervous system had just woken up.

That was the day I decided never to drink again. It also helped trigger my decision to say goodbye to working in China and return to Australia.

I don't know why the Chinese are so fond of alcohol in the professional or business environment, but it is a deeply embedded, nationwide phenomenon—at least it was before President Xi's anti-corruption campaign, which included targeting the drinking and gifting of ridiculously expensive Chinese alcohol (priced from several hundred yuan to over ten thousand yuan).

Before 2013 it was not uncommon for a small-group business dinner in Beijing or Shanghai to cost $10000—more than an average family in China earns in a whole year. The anti-corruption campaign and the closure of these luxury restaurants has ended much of the trade in super-expensive alcohol for gifting, but excessive alcohol consumption continues to haunt professional social life. Of course, they would spare most foreigners who are visiting China, but for any local Chinese (especially males), not to play the drinking games could be seen as arrogance and could lead to the nonconformist being banished from the table.

Those of us who have escaped the alcohol culture of China no longer have to worry about one threat to our health. Another friend, who is working for a property development company in Sydney, still has a drinking problem, however.

His work means he must frequently meet Chinese investors, who expect a seafood feast and expensive alcohol at the dinner table, where most of their business is negotiated and deals are made. These occasions are a lot less frequent than in China, but still they have placed a massive burden on his cardiovascular system. Apparently, the booming of the real estate industry in Australia, especially where it is funded by Chinese investors, has brought other features of Chinese business culture to Australia.

Not long ago I visited a Chinese restaurant in Sydney's Chinatown. What was very different about this Chinese restaurant was its layout. Most of the Chinese restaurants you find in Sydney, especially those that serve seafood, are of the traditional Cantonese style. They have a big open main hall with 10 to 20 tables, and a few smaller private dining rooms for groups. This new restaurant consisted only of private rooms, which was common in China before 2013. When businesspeople are entertaining government officials, they do not want to be watched by the public. The fact that this type of layout is now available in Sydney intrigues me.

Chatting with the waitress, I was not surprised to discover that the owner of the restaurant was the son of a high-ranking official working in the Chinese Consulate General in Sydney. I don't think these types of restaurants will become popular in Sydney, but it is interesting to note that they exist here now.

TIPS FOR WORKING WITH THE NEW CHINESE

Frequently, Australian employers checking the résumé of new Chinese job candidates, especially those who have arrived only recently and have not tailored their CV to the Australian standard, are surprised by the inclusion of so much personal information, such as date of birth, gender, marriage status, religion and even political affiliation. Some even attach photographs to their résumé. This seems strange to Australians, but it is actually a minimum requirement in China when submitting an employment résumé. I have explained to many of my mentees of Chinese background that they should not include any such information that could raise the potential for discrimination by employers.

But those Australian companies that are open to all job applicants should not be surprised when they see this type of résumé, and should not be too ready to question the professionalism of the applicant (unless applying for an HR job, of course). It may mean no more than that they are new to the job market and have not got used to local practices. Most applicants will soon realise their mistake and make the necessary changes.

Another interesting thing to note when meeting a Chinese applicant is that they often use an English name rather than the English form of their Chinese name. For example, 'Barry' has nothing to do with my Chinese name, as shown in my passport. It is simply a name I picked when I arrived in Australia so I did not have to explain how to spell or pronounce my name every time I met someone new.

There is no rule on how these names are created. Many Chinese prefer to use this English name in their résumé so it is easier for a potential employer to call them for interview. It is human nature that most people want to avoid pronouncing a name wrongly and would feel more comfortable with something simple and familiar. Many Australian-born Chinese (my children included) have their English names in their official documents. Other Chinese prefer to keep using their Chinese name, particularly if it is fairly easily pronounced by English speakers.

When interviewing overseas Chinese, you may well find that some of them don't speak English well enough. How important this is will depend on the job itself. For example, if you need someone to deal only with English-speaking clients or to fill a telemarketing role, then they are probably not the right choice. If you are hiring them mainly to serve tourists, their bilingual ability could be more useful to you than perfect English.

If you are hiring them to do bank reconciliation, an ability to communicate clearly enough should be sufficient for the job. Most Chinese professionals working in Australia have completed tertiary education, often with a master's degree. This is clear evidence that they can learn and improve quickly, including their spoken English, once they are part of your organisation.

In my opinion, typical new Chinese employees are easy to manage, given that they have been strongly influenced by the Confucian culture discussed in chapter 5, in which obedience to superiors is deemed a virtue. Among their peers, they act modestly and discreetly, which in most cases makes them pleasant co-workers. Of course, if the job primarily requires them to be outgoing and creative, this could raise difficulties, but my own industry prefers quiet achievers to loud talkers.

The Chinese are not silly, though. I have noticed in recent years that Chinese professionals in Australia are increasingly aware of their rights. They would not hesitate to ask for a pay increase (if in a soft manner) or the same working conditions as their Australian peers. Generally speaking, the longer they have lived in Australia, the more 'Australian' they will appear in all settings, including the professional work environment. In the not-so-common event that they become your boss, they will probably not behave very differently from any Australian boss you have had.

A friend of mine, who is 10 years older than me, works at IBM in Sydney as a very senior business manager. He is a new Chinese who was born in China and worked there until 2010. Although he has not lived in Sydney very long, his lifestyle is a lot more Aussie than mine. He runs 10 kilometres on Sundays and goes sailing and kayaking, activities a typical Chinese like me is unlikely to be interested in. And when I talk to him, I can see his mindset is quite western. As a Gen X Chinese, he definitely has a stronger affiliation to western culture than my generation on average, and therefore fits better into the Australian professional work environment.

My wife is another example of a new Chinese who has thrived in the Australian work environment. She has something in common with my friend at IBM. They both greatly admire western culture and lifestyles. In addition to things such as travelling, fishing and dancing, Zhen has a new hobby—baking cakes, like any Australian mum would get into with their kids. And unlike me (I still hold my Chinese passport), she never hesitated to give up her Chinese citizenship for an Australian passport, which can help her travel more freely in the world.

My wife's passion for western culture and ideas goes way back to when we first met in business school in China. She was a volunteer for AIESEC, the international student exchange organisation that had just started its operation in China. The interesting thing was that AIESEC was not operating with the necessary government approval in China, the Chinese government monitors all foreign not-for-profit entities very carefully, so they had to work under the government's radar. Most students like me would avoid it because of the potential risk and the tough English requirement. My wife, on the other hand, was extremely passionate about the cause and became the chairperson of the local committee on our campus. I suppose this speaks volumes about the differences in our personalities and cultural perspectives, and certainly it explains why she is doing better in her professional career in Australia than I am.

CHAPTER SUMMARY

- Young Chinese graduate job applicants are typically short on work and general life experience. They are professionally competent but may lack communication and other soft skills.

- Most Chinese professionals working in Australia are well educated, quick learners, easy to manage, and modest and discreet among their peers.

- Chinese professionals working in Australia frequently report an inability to break the bamboo ceiling that prevents them from moving up to management and leadership roles.

- Excessive drinking on work social occasions remains a deeply embedded cultural phenomenon in China, a problem that many new Chinese in Australia have left behind them.

- Generally, the longer new Chinese migrants live in Australia, the more 'Australian' they will appear in all settings, including the professional work environment.

CHAPTER 9

THE FUTURE

THE PROMISING BIG PICTURE

It was clear by 2016 that the Chinese economy was in big trouble. Even the government does not deny it anymore. Double-digit growth ended with the GFC and will probably never return. The real economy is struggling in the face of soft export demand and slow consumer spending growth, while property prices have soared to record highs because of large-scale speculative spending. After 30 years of hyper growth, it looks inevitable that China is heading into an economic downturn and perhaps a long-term recession like the one Japan has experienced since 1990.

Although I have studied economics at one of the best business schools in China, I really cannot pretend any confidence in analysing and predicting China's economic future. There are so many great economists looking at the Big Data and making predictions about China almost every day. Some of them were pretty negative about China's future a decade ago, but the country just kept growing. The accuracy of the trade and economic data coming out of China has often been open to question, but the money is real. Since October 2016 the Chinese yuan has been included in the Special Drawing Rights (SDR) basket of the

World Bank, which has further globalised the currency. This seems to indicate that China's growth and globalisation will continue, no matter how negative the economic news appears to be in some western media.

I think the future is as much about people's expectations as about economic realities. In my early years in Australia I read quite a few negative predictions about China. I enjoyed reading them, in the way that bad news always tends to be more exciting than plain good news. So my expectations for China were low. I was worried about the country's future and about the future of my parents, who would never leave China to join me in Australia. I was also worried about my own future, as my parents wanted so much to have me back in China. Although leaving China was a smart move for me, I cannot deny that the Chinese economy never did crash as some had predicted. And my parents are still doing fine in China.

Most people living in China today still have a strong belief in the future. And why should they not? They have witnessed with their own eyes the magical growth of their country since they were born. And they have devoted their whole life to helping build it. They have reason to be proud of what they have today, and to expect a better tomorrow. This optimistic picture is not hard to believe when living inside China and following the official state media every day.

The second season of *China's Mega Projects* released by China Central Television (CCTV) in October 2016 made exciting viewing. It showed that in the past 30 years China has built five times more roads than it had in 1976 and has built the world's largest highway system. There are now more than 120 000 kilometres of railway lines in China, including almost 20 000 kilometres of high-speed rail line built after the GFC, or about 60 per cent of all the high-speed rail currently existing in the world. With 20 000 tunnels and over one million bridges, Chinese roads and railways have tunnelled through mountains and spanned river systems to connect every remote corner of the country. With 230 airports and over 3.5 million flights, China has the world's second largest aviation network. Along its 32 000-kilometre coastline, China has built seven of the world's top ten ports. This huge traffic and the logistical network to support it alone make China the most special economy in the world.

But more important than these bare statistics is the psychological impact on hundreds of millions of Chinese who have watched it all happen. I felt inspired by the amazing achievements of the country after the GFC. I figured out that just maintaining these huge infrastructures year by year will probably cost more than the GDP of some small countries, not to mention China's ambitious plan to double the high-speed rail network in the next 10 years.

I still remember the sceptics when China first announced plans to build the high-speed train line in 2004. Although China was more than 20 years behind the developed world when it started the project, it has a larger market than the entire developed world combined, and it is still growing.

The ambitious plans this documentary outlined also reminded me how China has achieved its growth over the past 30 years. In a country such as Australia, where most property is privately owned, building a new railway line or expanding an airport or developing any kind of infrastructure requires lengthy public consultation and costly acquisition of private lands. As all land in Chinese cities is owned by the state, and all land in the villages is under collective ownership (controlled by the local Communist Party secretary), negotiating the most cost-effective land compensation is quick and easy.

Consultation and environmental considerations were almost nonexistent in the past. In recent years, because of the expressed concerns of a growing middle class about economic, social and environmental issues, the government has actually started public hearings and consultations on important infrastructure projects. Although the consultation is now more than just a formality, it is still far easier to push through such a project in China than in any other developed country in the world.

This is a great advantage of central planning and the one-party political system. The leaders do not always make the best decisions, but they can at least act much more quickly than their western counterparts. And sometimes quick reactions in a rapidly changing global environment are important. This has given the Chinese government a great competitive edge over western governments.

The real economy is in trouble due to rising labour costs and deteriorating market conditions, which actually gives China a great opportunity to reform and start a new chapter. As Jack Ma said in his recent speech about the Chinese economy, many companies will die in this round of recession, but others will soon rise. Taking a long view, I have no doubt that China will continue to grow, and there will be more and more opportunities in this country. I hold tight to this positive mindset because I am convinced that a positive mindset will help to create a more positive future.

THE WORRYING REALITY

Among the Chinese community in Australia, we generally find that the longer we stay overseas, the more positive we are about our home country. When we first came here we were looking for things that were simply not available inside China, such as better education, more interesting career opportunities or greater political freedoms. And we found these in Australia. So we started to compare China unfavourably with Australia in some respects. This was especially so for my generation. When we started to find out about those missing parts of our history that were not taught in China, many of us developed an anger towards the current regime and felt very negative about the country.

But after a decade in the developed world, we gained a better understanding of the western system and came to recognise that no country is perfect. One-party dictatorship is obviously not good, but democracy has its weaknesses and flaws too. The dramatic rise of President Donald Trump and the great uncertainty he brought to the United States and its allies (including Australia) is a good example of that. My gut feeling is that President Xi has more popular support inside China than President Trump has inside the United States. The Trump victory has caused many new Chinese to ask some hard questions about the western democracy they once admired.

The other important reason for the local Chinese community to become more supportive of China is its growing economic influence. I could never find the exact figure, but certainly a large number of people with a Chinese background work in industries related to China, such as property construction and sales, or *Daigou* (shopping agents for China). The boom in their home country has given them new career opportunities overseas. With more cash in their pockets thanks to the growth in their home country, they start to become supporters of China and to take less interest in the issues that once concerned them.

Returning to the country can reawaken these concerns, however. Although I consider myself to be very supportive, when I put myself inside the environment, I still find some of China's major problems very confronting. In December 2016 I travelled back to Beijing with my younger son to visit my parents. I was again shocked by the level of the pollution there, especially in winter when the city is heated by coal. The smog reduces visibility to less than 10 metres and turns bright day into dark night. A temporary inconvenience for me, hundreds of millions of people must cope with these severe conditions every day.

For the whole trip I restricted my son's outdoor activity to one short walk on the ice. When he started coughing I realised what a bad idea it was to be outdoors. I could keep him indoors for a week, an option not open to all the Chinese parents who live there. When the air pollution is bad, the hospitals are packed with sick children. Is it reasonable to expect their worrying parents to think only of their pride in China's magical economic development? They are probably thinking about how to migrate to a foreign country where their kids can grow up healthily.

This is not just an environmental issue. It is also a serious problem of human resources. The unsustainable environment is driving many talented professionals and wealthy businesspeople out of the country. This is probably the biggest threat to the future of China. Despite its huge population, after 30 years of the one-child policy China is already approaching the turning point of population growth. If most of the smart and successful people decide to leave the country, who is going to build China's future? But of course I don't have the right to ask this question and pretend I'm being patriotic, because I have already run away from the problem.

While the Chinese government can't stop talented people from leaving China, they do have the power to stop money from leaving the country. In January 2017, China introduced a stricter foreign exchange and transfer policy, which has effectively put a pause on globalisation of the Chinese currency. But more interesting than the foreign currency control itself was the way the Chinese government was going about it.

Unlike in Australia, where an important public policy shift like this would go through public hearings and parliamentary debate, and probably take months if not years to become enforceable, in China it can happen overnight. The stricter policy on foreign exchange for private citizens was announced on 1 January 2017 and took effect from 1 January 2017. Before this, Chinese citizens could freely exchange US$50000 per year; since 1 January, although the $50000 quota remains, any foreign exchange would require an application to the foreign exchange regulator under the central bank. The application will require a statement of purpose and may not be approved. More importantly, it is strictly prohibited for private individuals to exchange money for the purpose of investing in foreign countries—including through property purchase. Most people didn't learn this until 2 January because of the New Year holiday.

This change will have a profound impact on middle-class and rich Chinese, especially those keen to migrate overseas as professionals or investors. It is now much harder to send money out of China through legal channels, and the government strikes on underground banks have made the illegal channel a lot riskier too.

I suspect this change in Chinese foreign currency regulation will have great impact on Australia's property market too, especially for off-the-plan apartments. A large number of new apartments have been approved and sold to Chinese buyers over the past years. Most are due for completion and settlement in the next two years. Since Australian banks have already put a stop to loans via foreign-sourced income, where will these foreign buyers get money to settle their property?

Many of these buyers may lose the 10 per cent deposit they have already paid, if they can't send the balance out of China. In the past it was possible for those with a big family to have each family member send out their US$50 000 quota. Now they would need hundreds of relatives and friends to send small amounts of money out (for the purpose of overseas travel or study, for instance). It's very hard to imagine that they could do this undetected, given the Chinese government's access to cloud monitoring and Big Data analytic technologies.

I don't imagine these Chinese who are about to lose a fortune will feel very positive about China and its policy-making system. Yes, it is very efficient and effective, and it does not affect the majority of Chinese people, who have no foreign currency to send overseas. But the inherently unpredictable nature of public policy raises the level of uncertainty of the middle class and the rich, which will further push them out of the country. Unchecked, this drain of talented and rich people can't be a good thing for the country.

In the end, I guess, whether we feel positive or negative about China's future will depend on where we ourselves stand. When outside China, I feel very positive; once I step inside the country, I can't wait to get back to Australia. But I also see many millions of people without the option of leaving who are determined to make their home a better place. I am a selfish citizen, in that I am above all concerned about my own children's health and safety, and I am not playing a direct part in fixing my home country. Yet it is also true that there are still many talented people inside China who have access to more opportunities because 'the selfish ones' have left. I have no doubt that they can do a better job than me, and that my family here need me more.

CHILDREN OF THE NEW CHINESE

My children are ABCs (Australian Born Chinese). I used to joke about my older boy, Nathan, who was conceived in China then came to Australia inside his mum's belly, being still technically 'Made in China' from 100 per cent Chinese material, only with an Aussie label (birth certificate). Regardless of where they were born, if a Chinese child came to Australia when they were young enough, they will certainly be more 'Aussie' than Chinese. There's another joke about the ABCs: they are called 'Bananas'—yellow skin, but white inside.

As the children of migrants, they will grow up in an Australian environment and fully adopt Australian values. They will speak English with a perfect Australian accent. If someone doesn't see them in person or read their last name, they would have no clue of their origin. I have met so many ABCs in this country. I envy them, because they enjoyed from the very beginning advantages that their parents had made possible through their hard work. They have parents and probably siblings to turn to when they need help, and as they grow up here all their best friends are here for them too.

What I have observed over the years, however, is that typical Australian Born Chinese are not very good at Chinese languages. Even if they speak Mandarin or Cantonese at home, their Chinese accent is sometimes hard for a native Chinese speaker to understand. And those few who do speak quite well almost never read or write Chinese. As a written language, it is much harder to learn than English, given there are at least 5000 characters to memorise before you can read the newspaper. A close friend of mine whose family was originally from Beijing can communicate pretty well on most topics, but can't understand Chinese television and news. He can write little more than his own name in Chinese. Having said that, I'm sure some ABCs have mastered the Chinese language, but it will have demanded at least 10 years of structured learning. For most ABCs, their parents didn't bother to spend too much time and money on this.

As my children grew, I came to realise how important it was for them to learn Chinese. Earlier migrants will have paid little attention to this. When they arrived in Australia decades ago, China was a poor country and Chinese an unimportant language. They wanted their children to become Australians, a true part of the Australian society. I understand that. I too want my children to feel like real Aussies, but we are living in a different world now. China's rise is only just beginning. Chinese (in particular Mandarin) will become a more and more important language globally. Is it wise for my children to give up the language, especially given the very strong cultural ties we have and their access to the tools for learning this language?

Thinking about this, I realised that the new generation of ABCs will be quite different from previous generations. There must be many new Chinese migrants thinking like me. Unlike their own parents, the younger generation of parents not only value education but also place a greater value on cultural ties to mainland China. Yes, we think education is important, but we also have much more wealth to spend compared with earlier generations of migrants. This is evidenced by the soaring property prices in suburbs where top-ranked public and private schools are located. It is also demonstrated by the large number of tutoring centres in or around the Chinese suburbs. As for the Chinese language, there are already community schools teaching Mandarin everywhere, and there will be more in the future.

My generation of Chinese migrants worry about our children's future in a competitive global environment. We have the language skills that enable us to work in both China and the English-speaking world, while our children could lose out on the opportunity to work in China or in China-related settings. On the other hand, young children who never leave China will learn great Chinese *and* to speak fluent English. Parents in China devote much more time and money to their children's English-language education than we do on our children's Chinese-language education.

Perhaps my children will never go back to China to work or do any work related to China. But in 20 years' time, when the new generation of Chinese migrants arrive in Australia, my children's only competitive advantage would be their authentic Aussie accent. Who knows what the world will be like in 20 years' time? I certainly don't want them to hold me responsible for not giving them enough education, especially when I already foresee some of the challenges they may have in their life (and the opportunities they might miss out on if I don't act).

The other difference between the new ABC generation and the previous ones is their travel record to China. As we all have parents or grandparents and other relatives still living in China, and travel to China these days is both uncontrolled and affordable, we return to mainland China with our children much more regularly than previous generations of migrants. So our children will inevitably be more influenced by modern Chinese culture than their predecessors.

Meantime popular culture from mainland China is on the rise in Australia too. In times past it was impossible to find mainland Chinese television, films and music in Australia. Now they can be found in all Chinese suburbs and even in mainstream shops and cinemas where there are lots of international students. Many of my Aussie friends enjoy watching the Chinese dating show *If You Are the One* on SBS more than I do. I was surprised to find a kids' show produced by CCTV on ABC4 the other day. This trend is likely to continue.

CAUGHT BETWEEN AUSTRALIA AND CHINA

I remember a scene from a Canadian TV show about some super-rich second-generation Chinese living in Vancouver where she said how much she loved Vancouver. She described Vancouver as a city caught between Canada and China, which perfectly mirrored how she felt about herself. I doubt I will ever have that much money, but I totally share her feeling of being caught between two countries.

Typical and very traditional Australians will never really see me as an Australian; most Chinese will also see me as very different from them. I think I understand the mindset of both sides, but it will take a huge effort for both sides to understand and accept who I am. Even the parents who gave me life needed many years to accept my decision to live permanently in Australia. And I am far from alone. Like all new Chinese migrants caught between Australia and China, we love this country and we enjoy our life here.

Living in a city such as Sydney, where over 7 per cent of the population is of Chinese origin, I feel like I have never quite left

China. There has not been a single day in the past five years that I have not met someone of Chinese appearance. More than half of all Chinese restaurants in Australia are located in Sydney, and more than half of my dining out is spent in them. I could survive a week without going to Coles or Woollies, but I'd find it very difficult not to visit a Chinese grocery. There is actually a greater variety of foods in a Chinese grocery in Sydney than in Beijing, because the Chinese in Sydney have come from all over China.

Doing what I do—accounting—means more face time with Chinese than in other occupations. Because of the large number of Chinese overseas students studying accounting in Sydney over the past decades, and of Australian-born Chinese also studying accounting, there are simply more Chinese faces in my profession than in any other. Many of my colleagues are Chinese; many of my clients are too. Often I have to explain a professional topic in Mandarin to help my client understand better. This would have been unimaginable for the last generation of Chinese to escape China for Australia.

It has been eight years since I left university. Earlier this year I enrolled for a new master's degree at the University of New South Wales majoring in marketing. I thought there would be fewer Chinese in marketing than in accounting. The percentage of Chinese students was lower in the marketing major, yet still at least half of the students in the classroom were Chinese. And, just as I did eight years ago, I get to discuss the assignments and team projects with my classmates in Mandarin.

Besides work and study, I have been volunteering for CPA Australia, the country's largest professional body for accountants. In 2016 I was elected deputy chairman, and have since become chairman, of the Young Professionals Committee for New South Wales. We organise events and provide assistance to CPA members under the age of 35. Guess who the majority of all the members are, and in particular the younger members?

You're right, Chinese. So again, when I provide advice and coaching to young members for their professional development, I use Mandarin much of the time.

You can see that the experience I have today is distinctly different from the experience of previous generations of Chinese migrants to Australia. They never had so many people of similar background around them, so they tended to stick together and build their own community in Chinatown. It helped them to retain their identity and stay connected with their own people. Today Chinatown is nothing more than an entertainment centre, with restaurants and karaoke bars its main draws.

With advances in technology, the new Chinese migrants do not have to travel to Chinatown to connect to their original culture. They can simply turn on their mobile and connect directly to China and their own version of Chinese culture. And with air travel becoming so easy and affordable, they can fly back to China pretty much anytime they like (provided they are not blacklisted by Chinese border security).

My one big problem today, as I have already shared, is soaring house prices. And that has everything to do with the Chinese as well. It is true that the Chinese are far more obsessed with property purchase than any other ethnic group living in Sydney. The worst part is that most of them have a lot more money than I do! But I am not too worried. The economy goes in circles, and so do house prices. By focusing on my own professional development, I know that one day I will be able to find the ideal property for my family. I just need to wait for the market to cool down a little.

So five years since my 'escape', my life seems perfect. I have the ideal job, a lovely wife and two wonderful kids. I also have great hopes for the future. Living in this wonderful city caught between Australia and China, I have all the freedom I ever wanted and yet I don't have to disconnect from my original cultural background. It looks like I could 'live happily ever after', just like in the fairy tales.

But a fairy tale is fairy tale, and life is life. I have always known that someday new challenges would arise, although I did not expect them to come so early. Last year one of my cousins in China died of heart disease at the age of 40. His early departure had everything to do with the alcohol abuse I had escaped from. But I feel very sad for him that he never had a chance to get free of it.

In Chinese we have an old saying: 'Good luck seldom comes in pairs, but bad things never walk alone.' Which proved to be right again. Devastated by his son's death, my cousin's father—my father's older brother—was himself soon diagnosed with stomach cancer. Then my other uncle and an aunt, who had also lived all their lives in my hometown, were also diagnosed with cancer.

The pall of grief hanging over my family owed much to the succession of cancer diagnoses, one after another. But I believe that the heavy pollution of my hometown from so many years of coal excavation and related industrial waste discharge has had a calamitous impact on the health of the whole city. An article in a popular Chinese magazine in 2009 identified over 200 'cancer villages' in 27 provinces of mainland China. Most of these villages are located near industries with notorious environmental records.

More than 3 million people are diagnosed with cancer every year across China. Six people are diagnosed with cancer every minute; five people die of cancer every minute. Only since last year have I begun to understand how terminal illness and death threaten my family.

One day my parents will need me by their side. It is considered very unfilial for a Chinese son to send his parents to a retirement village. And I know my parents would not want to come to

Australia, because they have no friends here and do not speak English. I will soon face my biggest challenge in life—how to care for my aged parents. Compared with escaping from China to pursue a better life, this will most likely be the bigger challenge—for me and all the new generation of Chinese migrants in Australia.

CHAPTER SUMMARY

- The future is as much about people's expectations as about economic realities, and most people living in China today still have a strong belief in the future.

- The unsustainable environment is driving many talented professionals and wealthy businesspeople out of the country. This is probably the biggest threat to the future of China.

- The current ABC generation are growing up to be Aussies but risk losing their own culture, especially the Chinese language, which could disadvantage them in a competitive world in which China will play a growing role.

- Chinese migrants often feel 'caught between two countries': we love our adopted country, but continue to have deep cultural and personal ties to our homeland.

AUSTRALIA
27 FEB 2012
IMMIGRATION
SYDNEY
AIRPORT

AFTERWORD
BY MIKE LIANG

Like Barry Li, I'm also a new Chinese who took a similar journey to Australia. Because I'm a few years older than him, I thought I must know more about China myself. But when reading this book, I discovered many interesting facts and insightful observations. This book has refreshed my own understanding of my home country. Although this book is intended for general Australian readers who don't know a lot about China, I do believe every new Chinese should read it too.

We Chinese call ourselves the descendants of the dragons. It was a poor translation. The Chinese dragons are very different from the dragons in western myth. They don't guard treasures in dark caves or spooky castles. In Chinese legend, they live in rivers and oceans, and they fly high in the sky and bring people rain and good harvest. More interestingly, their appearance is a combination of Qilin's head (Qilin is another legendary animal in China, originating from African giraffes), a snake's body, a fish's scales and an eagle's feet. We now know this sacred creature was created by ancient Chinese as an animal totem. And this totem is a combination of all the different animal totems from the major ancient tribes in China, who speak different languages and favour different food. The Chinese dragon therefore is also a symbol of unity and harmony for all Chinese peoples.

Now the Chinese dragon is flying all over the world. Unlike the western dragon that blow fire and causes fear, the Chinese dragon dances on major holidays and races in Australia's rivers and harbours. Any fear and concern over China's growing economic and cultural influence in Australia, in my opinion, is unnecessary. For anyone who had those fears and concerns in the past, I strongly recommend you read Barry's book. This book explains well where the Chinese dragons came from and how they think, and more importantly, what they bring to Australia.

I've known Barry for a long time, but he still surprised me when he finished this book. Telling our stories is not easy, and I'm glad Barry did it well for all the new Chinese in Australia. I'd also like to take this opportunity to thank him for his contribution to the CPA profession and for assisting me to start the Association of Chinese Accountants Australia (ACAA). Barry has been long known as a passionate volunteer and an excellent young leader and now he is a great author too. I wish him the best and I hope all the readers enjoyed this book as I did.

Mike Liang FCPA,
Founder of the Association of Chinese
Accountants Australia (ACAA)

26 January 2017

INDEX

Printed in Australia
04 May 2018
672550

9 780730 351870